# From the
# Hood 2 Horses

## Freedom Zampaladus

From the Hood 2 Horses

ISBN: 978-1-910181-20-1

Published October 2015
First printed October 2015
Reprinted October 2015

Printed and Published by Anchorprint Group Limited

Enquiries:
The Urban Equestrian Academy Ltd
1 The Crescent, King Street, Leicester, LE1 6RX

Email: tfzampa@gmail.com

Website: www.hood2horses.co.uk

# CONTENT

# ACKNOWLEDGMENT

First, I would like to reach out to the Creator for without life I would not have been able to be thankful for all that I have, particularly my fantastic children. I am forever grateful for the mindset you have given me and the talents you have blessed me with and I acknowledge the love and affection provided no matter the trials and tribulations that face me on a daily basis. To you ALL praise is due.

To my immediate family, the children, I love you all equally and for sure each one of you have undoubtedly helped mould me into the person I am today.

To Virginia (Amani) Berkeley; wifey, my lioness; that you are! We have shared some great times and despite our struggles that love will always be their no matter what! Love u. I thank you for giving me and you beautiful children, with wonderful souls, spirits and manners. For sure you are and always will be No1.

To my Mother and Father, Love Eternal. For sure you have instilled in me the warrior spirit you all have; love you both very very much and appreciate the way you raised us indeed#NeverGonnaBeASlaveToTheSystem!!

To my brothers and sisters love you all. To my brother on holiday in particular 'Keep your Head up', life is full of twists and turns.

To my Wadadli family, love you all. Especially you Uncle whom I admire so much#RealTalk

To the Wints and rest of the family in the UK, Canada, Jamaica, the states and wherever else in the world, stay blessed, much love to each and every one of you also, keep winning.

To my team KINGZNUBIAN; Negus movements only!! Love and Light#9ToTheHighestPower

To my friends and those who believe in me, I believe in you. Thank you for your support, it does not go unnoticed and never will. I'm humbled by your support and will continue to do my best 'Inshallah'.

Lastly this book is for all those who wondered what happened when I left the UK back in 1994, well here it is.

It's also for anybody who has had a tough time or happens to be going through a tough time, remember there is always somebody going through worst. Stay humble, focused, pray and keep fighting the good fight!

This is 'Part One' of a Trilogy so I hope its worth me writing 'Part Two!'

To anybody who saw the title and purchased it based on possibly being an interesting read, thank you too.

Lastly; their is a story in each and everyone of you, go ahead and tell it.

Wasalaam

## FR33DOM

Though this is an autobiography, it is approximately 95% accurate. For a number of reasons the authentication has deliberately been falsified by that approximate 5%. Which 5% you will never know. Thanking you in advance for your overstanding.

# JUNGLE MASTERS

I was a bit of a nerdy kid growing up in the UK in that
I could literally tell you the name of a bird just from the
way it flew. With my first group of friends I formed a
crew called Jungle Masters and members were given an
animal nickname; I mean mine was Osprey for fuck sake.

I was however a popular kid, very athletic I was the
fastest runner in both primary and secondary school,
a keen basketballer in secondary, and apparently the
strongest, in primary school; an unwarranted title because
I personally always thought my mate Darren Kabengele
was the strongest though I never told him this, as I
realised quite quickly it was a good accolade to have.

I went to Moat Community College on Maidstone Road
which was not far from where I lived and enjoyed school
as our class was jokes, some funny characters. Gavin
Francis who was one of my best friends was simply loud,
he always had the freshest fades; Kedesha Joseph who
was a lovely girl, really tall she had a good heart and
fancied the pants off me; she would ask me out like every
other month; Mitesh Chohan my brother from another
mother and a true Hip Hop head, he introduced me to
gangster rap, the likes of N.W.A, Ice T and so on, we
would wind up the staff on the school buses playing this
music loud on our Walkman's.

I was at that age, 14; the age where you just want to
be around, those transition teenage years, where all
the after school fights tended to happen, where being
rebellious was the thing to do and life just seemed good;
I didn't want to go.

"Can't I stay here? Why do we have to leave for? Were
not really going init mum? Why?" These were the

questions running through my head since Dad said we were moving to Antigua.

Dad was a man who did not mince his words; if he said something he meant it and though I at first doubted we would move, everything was falling into place and it truly sank in when he stated he'd brought the tickets, sold his taxi and had put the house up for rent.

I remember the surreal feeling of saying goodbye to our family members and how we gave away a lot of our toys, the games console, our drum set; and explaining to our neighbours constantly how we were moving to the West Indies. It was sad times particularly for me and I'm sure Jaden my 13 year old younger bro, being that we were 'of that age'. Giving away our cat Cleo to Mrs B; how would Cleo get on? These were some of the things running through my mind at the time.

I can't remember much about my last day at school but I remember the Head teacher 'Mrs Hussain' encouraging me to 'keep my head up' because in her opinion I was a good student who would go on to do well and how the school would miss my character and a few weeks before my last day 'Mr Jenkins' explaining how, if I acted up over there, the 'teachers' would 'whoop my ass', that really pissed me off!

A memory that really stuck to this day was leaving on the night to catch that flight; saying goodbye to mum and sis; gazing at every street sign heading out of Highfields; Earl Howe Street; St Peters Road; Sparkenhoe Street; Maidstone Road and then the coach station and feeling angry and extremely sad.

I can't remember much else about my last few days in England other than what I've just explained and it was now time for a new chapter in my life......

8

# CELEBRITY STATUS

It was that hot you felt like you couldn't breathe; the journey on the way here was strange; one minute it was exciting in that, yeah, we was flying through the air; looking out the window and seeing absolutely nothing but empty blue sea, at times nothing but cloud, but then upon changing hemisphere; getting closer to Antigua; this stifling sauna like ferocious heat was at first irritating. Dad decided we had to make a spectacular entrance and dressed us in the most ridiculous suits, with the shoes, ties yeah the full shebang. Upon landing; coming off the plane and dripping with sweat, he ultimately saw sense in allowing us to at least remove our jackets.

I remember the airport being bright pink, tiny, and thinking 'Gosh this island must have only 100 people or so, this is nothing like our airport in England'. Everything looked and smelt so different, so clean, pure; tropical. As we came through customs I remember the service we received. Our excited friendly big broad smiles were greeted with a stern emotionless dead look.

"Where you coming from?" the customs officer said in a deep low slow tone

"England" my dad replied

"Wha you come fa" the customs officer responded

"To see mi mom" said dad.

After some basic checks that were quite frightening for a child we were allowed through customs into the rest of the airport, it was so small I was thinking to myself. Jaden was "muttering this aint no airport, with only one shop, what kind of airport is this?"

**10**

I agreed it really was weird.

Apart from being sticky with sweat we was hungry! Dad was pacing back and forward to a phone box calling my Uncle I think. I guess he was running late. We had come Antigua before in 1986 or so and so I knew of him but I didn't have a clue what he looked like or anything. All I knew was that he was apparently well respected and a 'Bad Man', which meant from where we came from, a 'good man', if that makes sense!

We had the most awful hotdog or suttin and I was annoyed because I'm sure it wasn't halal! I knew, had mum known we was eating this 'thing' she wouldn't be happy!

After what seemed an eternity a well-dressed young Rastafarian turned up in a very smart convertible Saab. I didn't know who he was and why he was staring at us with these big eyes and this massive smile across his face. This dude had some serious swag; he had the coolest laid back confident walk I'd ever seen as he approached us and seemed to know everybody. It seemed as if he was a well-known person as people were smiling at him, shouting his name, and rushing to his assistance as if he was a celebrity.

"Uncle Levi" the Rastafarian said in an America accent.

Dad looked at him with a broad smile and greeted him with the typical blackman hug and fist bump action, "Wha a gwan Rasta man, which one you be; Jah Bless?"

"Yeah man, a me Ashton" the dreadlocked young man acknowledged.

# WHICH ONE A FREEDOM

So this is where Dad and his side of the family came from. This is where Dad was born; Seaton's' Village.

It turned out the Rastafarian lad who picked us up was in fact my cousin Uncle Oxcile' son, Ashton Tonge or Jah Bless as he now liked to be called. He was a cool dude. He seemed to be in a different zone, constantly smiling and laughing; happy, charismatic. Again, everybody seemed to know who he was with him constantly beeping everybody as we passed through the streets on our way to our new home. The journey from the airport to Seaton's was not too far, but having just arrived, everything obviously seemed real alien; so surreal.

The setting was so different; firstly everybody was black! It was strange to see so many black people everywhere doing everything. Driving, walking the roads, on their veranda's and oh yeah the houses, they all seemed to be bungalows and separate. Some houses looked quite nice but then as we passed through some streets many houses looked run down. Every single house had corrugated tin like roofs and many were made entirely from wood or partly wooden.

"So Freedom, Jaden" Jah Bless said on the way.

"How y'all doing, the flight was good?"

"Yeah alright I guess" we would hesitantly reply not knowing quite how to respond.

**13**

"Boys, Jah Bless, Ashton is your cousin; him and him brudda Marlon, me remember dem when they was little boys, yeah man dem get big now" Dad filled us in.

It was strange being called 'Freedom' over here; back in England only the elders called me by my middle name 'Freedom'; to everybody else I was simply Levi as in Levi Jr. To make things even more fucked up; amongst my family and friends back in the UK everybody called me LT, and to this day I still don't even know why, but over here in Antigua to our family and friends I was 'Freedom'; the name my Dad called me by and since our last visit to the Island it's all anybody over here had known me as; so though it was strange to me it wasn't to them.

"A Freedom this one", "Which one a Freedom", "Freedom and Jaden" everybody sounded so strange, this was all I heard constantly all day from these strangers who consisted of family members and friends; yeah literally rinsing out my name! So annoying.

Upon arrival there must have been about 20 people waiting for us; as we pulled up to the yard 2 men immediately raced to the gates and opened them for Jah Bless to roll straight through onto the pathway in the yard; it was like we was royalty.

One by one everybody would introduce themselves. Dad seemed to know most people. Apparently, we had 2

**14**

particular spots in Seaton's; our Uncles spot this place, which really was the family house and was where we were going to stay; and Aunt Cassie' which was on the other side of the village; this was where Grandma lived.

Uncle's spot or the family yard was a gorgeous gigantic bungalow; impressive design of wood and masonry in equal measure. It was surrounded and fenced in by a humongous garden which featured the 2 biggest mango trees in the village, about 7 coconut trees and many other fruits trees I was yet to find out about.

A few people stood out after our introductions; Rina who was our Uncles Wife and her children, twin's Che' and O'Shae, who were about 9 years old, Junior who was about 6 and Jarome who was coming on 2. They all seemed really nice; upon first introductions.

Rina showed us around the house, which room we were to stay in and so on; as it was just us at the time Dad wanted us to sleep in the same room with him, which was weird because me and Jay had always had our own room. Everything seemed so well organised, we were comfortably looked after, everybody was really nice but something still didn't seem right. Despite everything something still seemed like it was missing; and that's when it clicked; where was our Uncle?

# THE VILLAGE

A few hours must have passed now and we still were waiting on our Uncle to arrive.

"Don't worry the Don a come" was all everybody kept saying as we got to know each other.

It turned out "The Don" was Uncle's nickname, nobody really called him by his real name; "The Don" in fact became his real name and anytime it was mentioned it often generated a burst of excitement from whoever was mentioning it.

"The Don always busy you know star but trust me when him roll in he go roll in!!"

"Ta rass wha you nuh ketch he yet? Bwoy he nuh easy, he a come star nuh worry yuh self he a come, im appy fi hear you reach mon, big broda reach mon, big broda reach" a rather big man said, I wasn't sure who he was but I remember he was quite scruffy; holding a rather large machete and thinking to myself what the hell does he use that for!

I remember one particular individual; he was so so ugly!; face bumpy, with big boils, an absolutely unkept afro, uneven teeth and style of clothing I just could not work out. 'Gully Dawg' people kept calling him so I figured that was his nickname. This guy was super animated whenever it came to mentioning Uncle and I'd later in my life get to understand he was a key figure/ one of the few men in Uncles circle, whom Uncle trusted. Dad was in

**17**

his element obviously; he seemed so happy to finally be back home amongst his fellow bredrin and sistren; fellow Antiguans.

In relation to Antigua its original name pre – Columbus was Wadadli and as such it was commonplace to hear locals preferring to call the island by its original name, particularly those who were more cultural in tune. Antigua is in fact a twin island with the island of Barbuda being its twin; this smaller island's pre – Columbus name is in fact Wa' omni. In my time of living over here I would never actually get to visit Barbuda though would come to know it had many unique features such as a beach with pink sand, deer, wild boar and other things.

It turned out that Uncle wasn't going to make it until even later than how late he had already been and so Dad decided he would take us to go see our Grandma at Aunty Cassie's house the other side of the village.

Rather than get a lift there; Dad decided that we should walk. One of our cousin's whom we had just met came along with us, his name was Maurice but everybody called him Cashew Nut; he was another of my Uncle's sons about 18 and again had what seemed like a permanent smile on his face from the short time I'd known him.

Back to Dad, yep this was our Dad; he was back home in his element and so 'of cooourse' he'd want to walk through 'his village' on the way to Aunty Cassie's.

**18**

"A who dat Captain", "A Jahlis over de so, a wha you a say Jah man".

"Freedom, Jaden dis a your cousin Fenke".

You see Dad had been away for just under 40 years and so this was how he was going on; he was so proud he was back home and so proud to show off his two little men.

Walking through Seaton's, there didn't seem much. Sporadic houses here and there in close proximity, but all independent of each other. At times you could now smell the sewage in the gully's which ran at the side of the roads mixed with the heat this was a most vile smell. Someone was burning something as I remember smelling fire and thinking 'you can't just burn stuff like that in England', I remember many faces just staring at us as we walked through the village, sometimes 3, 4, 5 people together literally just staring usually emotionless with a "Good afternoon" and nod of the head by my Dad to acknowledge them if he didn't at first know who they were.

This was always of course followed up with a 'who dem dey Cashew Nut', with Cashew Nut thus explaining who they were, going back usually 2 generations so Dad could familiarise himself with the family tree as best he could.

**19**

# MY SON HAS RETURNED

As touched upon I'd always been fascinated by wildlife. The wildlife I'd seen over here in these few hours was mind blowing; I'd already seen loads of lizards, a couple humming birds, donkeys, some other weird looking birds and I was sure to see much more. The only animals that weren't so amazing were the pet dogs I'd seen; they all looked like mongrels and like they were dying!

"Look ur Aunty Cassie house over deh so, just down so" said Dad

A couple youngsters were in the yard observing us as we got closer and closer. Once close enough they rushed indoors; you could literally hear the excitement as they sounded out the rest of the household regards our imminent arrival. "Aunty Cassie, Aunty Cassie them a come them come!!" At first I was wondering, how did they even know who we were, but then remembered people were expecting us and obviously Cashew Nut was guiding us; still smiling.

I noticed Aunts house was really big, downhill and a strange shape. This was one of the few houses in the village where you had to climb a mountain of stairs to get up to the front door. So yeah; you had to go downhill, up some stairs, to get to the front door.

"Welcome back big brother, praise the Lord you mek it safely, your looking well", a strong female voice greeted us. Aunty Cassie was a well-built woman who's aura commanded respect. "Lovely to see you again sister you're looking well too, it's been much too long, much too long". The 4 youngsters turned out to be 'Ramiah (13), Azeezah (15), Likkle Barber (8) and Shamel (10)' they were our cousins. After warm embraces, we were welcomed into the household to see Grandma.

Grandma hadn't picked up on the commotion regarding us arriving. She was round the back and due to this being quite an emotional reunion particularly between her and her son, my Dad, we decided to surprise her. It had been 8 years since she had last seen him and some 40 years since he left the island. Aunty Cassie led the procession to the rear of the house to where she was.

Grandma was scrubbing some clothes as we quietly approached her out of sight. "Kiki; look who is here!" said Aunty; grandma with her back turned to us didn't hear Aunty at first and so didn't respond. "Kiki" she said again; "Kiki a you dat" Dad interrupted in a louder but soft tone. Immediately, Kiki stopped scrubbing, "a who dat" she said whilst turning around to acknowledge us.

"A wha you no hear me a come back home mommy". Emotionless, about 6ft from each other Kiki looked deep into Dads eyes as she tried to make sense of the situation, she looked at me dressed smartly, Jaden, and then back at Dad.

"Praise Jeeesus; my son has returned; Levi", she said, breaking out in the most radient of smiles followed by the most loving embrace.

# GRANDMA KIKI

She was ever so small, my Grandmother, again I'd met her on our previous visit but couldn't remember how she looked. She had strong Nubian features; had never ever left Wadadli whilst it was said she could probably accurately tell you the history of the island so vividly that her accounts and descriptions of 'how it used to be' were recorded and archived by the national museum for future generations, researchers and the like to use in discussion, work and so on.

Seaton's Village was close to 'Betty's Hope' slave plantation complex which was today used as a tourist attraction. Grandma would explain to us how things used to go there being that it was so close to the village for example how her mother used to get leftover meat from the plantation owners back in the day. This meat usually consisted of the waste parts of an animal, the parts the white man wouldn't eat, for example, the tail, feet, intestines and so on. This was why, we as Caribbean people were to become experts in utilising these parts of the animal; yeah that's right, Chicken and Lamb foot soup, Oxtail, Black Pudding just to name a few delicacies eaten today.

We must have stayed for a few hours at Aunts, Grandma so proud to have everybody home, overwhelmed with joy, couldn't stop acknowledging how big we were now. She also expressed her delight that Dad had got rid of our dreadlocks which we had since birth and upon our last visit.

Antigua is predominantly a Christian country. Grandma was a seriously religious Christian elder and there was always a stigma in relation to the Islands main religious populations views on Rastafarianism; even though we

**24**

had actually always been Muslim for many years we had dreadlocks I believe for cultural reasons.

"So you go send dem di school over deh? It's a nice school, you go have to get dem uniform and get dem books and so from town. Dem so big and handsome, dem look so much better wid dem hair sort out, little gentlemen, how me love dem so bad so so bad"

Whenever we managed to slip away from Grandma's grasp and questioning, we would slide into further questions from our 4 cousins.

"Wha mek Uncle Levi name u so?, Where ur sister dey?, Wha mek dem never come?, When dem a come?, Seaton's school u go go? A true you come fi live?, Wha England like?"

A lot of what they said didn't even register I mean that was too much patois for us and their accents were strong. It usually took our cousins a few attempts to get their question across which made things even more awkward. We had to explain so much I'm surprised we didn't get jaw ache at the time.

Naturally being a teenager I was drawn to Azeezah and Ramiah in conversation and left Jaden to occupy the younger two. Not that I didn't talk with them just that I was the centre of attention of the other too.

I remember Azeezah constantly telling me "U go get plenty girls you know, them go love you, a so you look good", she would say the same things over and over but just rearranged in different ways. Naturally I was intrigued but having to take in so much in these first few hours of arriving, 'girls' were the least of my worries!

**25**

# THE FAMILY YARD

It must have been a couple of hours we were at Aunt Cassies. There was still a lot to do, we had still to unpack and many other people to still get to know. Dad decided we had been at our Aunts long enough for now and so we said our goodbyes though intended to pass back later. Shamel decided he was coming with us and so tagged along.

Azeezah was still buzzing with the fact that she had got to question me first and I could see she was well chuffed at having new 2 cousins come to live whom she was plotting to share with her friends.

Little Barber wanted to come but he was deemed to be too young. Whilst at Aunties, Cashew Nut had disappeared, safe in the knowledge that having guided us to Aunts, Dad was confident in making his way back to the 'Family Yard'.

The journey on the way home was short and easy just a few turns and twists and a couple long roads. The weather was still absolutely piping and a few stops to some shops was necessary to get the refreshments needed. Each time we stopped at a shop Dad had to explain who he was or the owner already kinda knew. In our village I'd come to know there were 4 main shops. Mrs Welsh, Tizzy's, Annette's and 1 other.

Having got back to the yard a few people had now gone, but there were still quite a few. The Ugly dude was still there, as was Jah Bless who was chilling with some guys I didn't notice when we arrived, he was smoking what looked like a massive cigar, red eyed and still smiling politely he clocked us before we clocked them.

A few hours had again passed and it was now you could say early evening. By now I had worked out that besides the main bungalow, there was another half built wooden house in the garden as well as another two storey building, yes the first two storey building I had noticed on the island in our yard, which was a salon; in fact it was Rina' Salon and very pretty at that. There was a car underneath a car cover in the garage and a Honda Legend, beautiful car, parked in the yard which also belonged to Rina. There was also the SAAB which Jah Bless was driving. Even after all these objects the yard was still massive.

The yard itself consisted of a beautiful front veranda made of wood and stone and round the back of the house another smaller wooden veranda for Uncle's room with a spinning hanging basket chair you could sit in whilst on the veranda. All of the windows had gauze like netting and I later would understand these were to keep out what I would call the 'Demon Flies', I'll explain that later! It was a three bedroom bungalow and the design on the inside of the house was as stunning as the outside; wooden design split up with stone masonry. I was thinking this house is 10 times better than any house I'd seen in England, wow.

It was about this time that I hear what sounded like a dog barking and looking outside though our bedroom window I noticed hidden amongst the jungle of a garden a dog house with a rather funny looking medium sided dog.

# FLEA BITTEN

"That's Gringo, don't touch him he will bite you and don't get to close he's covered in fleas" said Che'. Everybody said they were identical and though they were, I could tell the difference through subtle minute details. For example Oshae' had a peak to his lip and fuller face to Che who himself had a more oval head shape.

"He is a Pit-Bull you know; dem have dem in England?"

"What's a Pit – Bull?" I responded. Me and my family were not really into dogs because we were Muslim though I'd always been a jealous kid who was jealous of those who did have them; we had cats.

The dog I noticed was really skinny and looked like it needed food; it was tied to a long metal chain.

"Don't get too close, fleas a go bite you, him have fleas, him kin wan wash" Oshae warned standing from a distance. I didn't really get what he was trying to say as again we were cat people and though we knew what fleas were, it only registered when about 30 seconds after Oshae said what he said I felt a sharp burning sensation on my hand.

"Argghh!!, what the fuck"

"See me tell you, flea a bite you, move from deh man move from deh and brush off!". I soon realised what he was saying and started frantically brushing myself off whilst retreating from the area in case any more fleas happened to be on me. These biting jumping little critters were so small and difficult to kill when u did spot one that if you didn't squeeze them with authority they were gone in a flash.

Dusk was approaching now and it was quite a beautiful sight. Seeing the different hues of the sunset in a tropical environment, really made you appreciate nature; and also brought home the reality that this was not England; but our new home. It was quite a surreal experience. "Good evening good evening" a man on a donkey said whizzing past the yard with a big load of sugar cane and another large machete; I guess that's why they had them for chopping sugar cane.

It was quite a funny sight because I'd only seen donkeys at Skegness in England and on those occasions' kids would ride them; here was a big man on a donkey with a large bundle of sugar cane, his toes were almost scrapping on the ground. I was thinking surely the guy is too big for that poor donkey! I could hear horses neighing from a distance too.

We were all around the front of the yard, still with a few people, when we could hear music from further up the road getting louder and louder. Everybody started getting animated.

"The Don a come nuh, look your Uncle a come" Gully Dawg stated smiling.

At that moment an eerie silence fell around us as a stunning white jeep blasting reggae music ghostly pulled up to the gate. Immediately as if automatic, Gully Dawg and another member of the yard party sprung to action opening the gates for the white jeep to enter the yard.

It really was stunning; the wheels were massive with chrome rims and trimming and blacked out windows so you couldn't see a thing through them. At this point the only thing you could hear was the monster engine purring whilst everybody was just staring at the jeep smiling. It was crazy, I mean I was itching to see my Uncle too but now I felt slightly anxious.

The engine stopped while the music was lowered. The front passenger door opened first and a man of medium build in a shirt, shorts and a baseball cap stepped from the vehicle.

Whilst this was happening, the front driver's side window lowered.

"A you dat Rasta" said the driver staring smiling at Dad, with teeth glistening it was him; 'The Don'.

# THE DON

He was only about 5ft 9ins, a short stocky man, but you could tell he was a special guy with a lot of money.

The clothes he was wearing, his jeep, his jewellery which included a diamond earring, a number of gold and diamond rings, Rolex watch and two front gold teeth with diamonds in literally spelling his name across his smile, you knew this was a serious dude! He literally smelt of money!!

"Zampaladus" Uncle sounded with a light chuckle approaching Dad as they embraced in a warm brotherly blackman hug.

"Bwoy a dem big vehicle you a push deh Jah man", dad asked Uncle with both laughing loving. It was like we were royal with Uncle and ourselves the Celebrities.

Dad seemed to be so happy to see his little younger brother, stepping out in style and looking well and likewise Uncle seemed real happy to see his big brother after all these years. I mean though they were brothers they had literally grown up without each other for most of their life's and the talk between them was that 'bigger tings were to gwan' now my Dad was on the scene.

"Dem look after you?" Uncle would say, referring to the people in the yard with a nod to acknowledge everybody who caught his eyesight.

"Where Rina dey, call she for me" Uncle ordered, with one of the twins immediately scattering to get her.

"So where the children dem, where Freedom and Jaden; come yah?" he instructed mentioning us, catching our gaze.

**34**

I remember being slightly nervous going over to greet him due to this aura of authority he seemed to demand; he seemed however a very friendly and polite man, just very acutely aware of his status as a boss figure.

"Hi Uncle" I would say

"Freedom! You get tall man; every ting alright?" Uncle greeted putting his fist out for a fist bump, gripping my head and shaking it.

"Yeah Man" I would respond trying to act cool but fucking crapping myself; I'm sure Jaden felt the same way.

You see he had these light hazel brown eyes unlike our Dads and his stare was cold; I felt uneasy looking into his eyes. He was clearer than Dad and those Gold teeth with diamonds in, spelling his name were, though fascinating; somehow made me feel on edge; oh yeah and the fact of being told constantly that he was a 'Bad Man' and him now seemingly justifying it.

In between periods of happy reflection with Dad; introducing Dad to everybody who was in the yard and who would pass through the yard; all the whilst giving orders to a number of individuals in the yard; Uncle would glace over at us and flash a smile seemingly reassuring us everything would be ok. This sense of being under his gaze slowly felt reassuring that we were in his circle and minute by minute it was beginning to feel ok in his presence. This was the thing just from his body language he somehow made us feel special.

"Which one a you like car? Mookie! You show dem di Porsche?"

This was Uncle he was asking me and Jaden if anybody had shown us his Porsche! Yeah the car underneath the car sheet in the garage was a Porsche!

'God's sake' I thought to myself, 'How much money does this guy have!'

"No no we no show dem boss" muttered one of the members of the yard as he scamper to remove the car sheet. I guess he must have been Mookie.

Removing the car sheet revealed a 'Black Porsche Carrera 911 convertible'. Wow I'd never been so close to such an expensive car; I thought the jeep was enough let alone sharing the yard with a 'Porsche Carrera'. Jaden was smiling from ear to ear as Uncle let us sit in the car and have a nose around, bro was well into cars. We both used to collect matchbox cars like most boys our age at the time so we knew about hot cars, speedsters and the like. Though I was into cars, I wasn't as crazy about them as Jaden was.

It was dark now and I was slightly frustrated because I didn't get to hear about or see uncle's racehorses. I knew Uncle had horses because Dad had always told us about them; one called Monster Mike in particular; you see my Dad was a big Mike Tyson fan as were we during the years when Tyson was at the peak of his career, as was Uncle and apparently he had named one of his horses after the famous boxer. We had also travelled to Coventry before we left England to purchase a horse trailer for uncle's raceyard and had packed it full with stuff so we didn't have to pay duty on our bits and shipped it over; this would arrive in a few weeks.

"Which one of you is the animal man, a Freedom a de animal man ent it?" Uncle asked as if telepathically reading my thoughts.

"Dem show you de horse dem?" He added.

"Erm no Uncle" I responded shyly.

"Ok well in the morning me will tek you to see the horse dem cah it's late now ok" he stated flashing that smile.

"Alright, thank you" but it wasn't alright I wanted to see them now!

**37**

# DEMON FLIES

**Mosquitoes** *scientific name: Culicidae; the females of most species are ectoparasites whose tube-like mouthparts pierce the hosts' skin to suck blood.*

My definition; Demon Flies!!! These terrible terrible little winged creatures that prey on humans during the night!! They have a deep attraction to foreign blood, buzz right into your earhole making the most irritating of sounds, suck your blood every and anywhere, leaving you with bumpy violently itchy skin the following day.

We got introduced to these insects on our first night; it turned out that we didn't have the right equipment so to speak to ward off these little bastards. The twins had warned us about them with a wry smile to their faces. "Mek sure you have plenty coil you know or else moskita a go bite you up, mommy left plenty for you". The twins revelled in briefing us.

We struck up quite a bond with the twins that night over dinner. We ate with them what was a fantastic meal. Macaroni cheese, rice and peas, yam, calaloo, potatoes fried dumplings, coleslaw, salad with feta cheese, marinated lamb slices and chicken, the tastiest chicken I'd ever had I must say. Rina was a great cook, better than mum I would think to myself and on this occasion I wasn't even concerned whether it was halal or not!

Mosquito coils were only so effective and as such our sleep was well interrupted by these irritating monsters. We must have had about 7 of these coil things in the room burning during the night before we went to bed and yet still it fell like an army of mosquitos were attacking you from the skies as soon as the lights went out. You could literally feel them land on you and as soon as they did, I'd try and squish them by slapping myself wherever I felt them land, obviously often missing.

It's like the fuckers were having a feast. Jaden was the same, moaning from getting bitten. Dad didn't come to bed so early he was out until early hours with the adults making one heap of noise on his first night home. Me and bro must have stayed up for most of the night with the light on trying to kill as many demons as we could. The more we killed the more that came our way. It was fun at first but then became rather tedious when we realised we weren't getting anywhere. Squashed mosquitoes and splats of blood all over the walls was quite a sight.

The sounds at night were quite amazing too, crickets we were told, yes the sounds of crickets in the night were very impressive, not to mention the bats that could be spotted due to the yard lights, they nestled in the mango trees and really came alive at night, how big they were.

All the time you could look out the window and spot a person or two simply posted as if strategically, usually always smoking that funny looking cigar, cigarette.

In the end me and my bro simply snuggled up together in the same bed under the covers where somehow we managed to get to sleep after a ferocious battle, the first of many that were to occur for our first few months in our new home.

# M16 NOZZLE AT UR DRAWS

Whenever reminiscing the morning after our arrival, a tune always starts to play in my head; Beenie Man's 'Murderer'; the lyrics went something like this……

"How would you feel if you wake up one morning and saw, a big M16 nozzle at your jaw"……..

Not that this is what happened to us, well not quite anyway.

It must have been like 6am, there was so much commotion I was thinking for so early. Uncle came busting into our room I was surprised that for so early he looked fresh and was fully clothed, dad was lying down in the bed next to us having got in early hours, slightly bemused.

"Zampa dem fucking babylon dem wan ask you some question, no worry bout nuttin u seen. Dem love fi give man problem and mus a hear say you land, see dem yah. Freedom, Jayden nuh worry bout nuttin you hear, everything is alright you see me"

We knew this had something to do with the police because looking out the bedroom window we could see loads of police in full gear with helmets and big massive guns searching the yard. Gully Dawg and a few others had to stand against one of the garden walls during the search. Within a few minutes of Uncle ranting, a policeman who looked like the boss man due to his badge, called Dad out of our bedroom.

"Don't worry yuh self boys I'm just going to have a few words with your father" the officer said; we just nodded.

As dad left, another policeman came into our bedroom with his machine gun and literally just positioned himself against the bedroom wall, holding his gun pointed to the ground, staring at us. I'd never seen such a big gun, Jaden neither.

"So where you all coming from England" the policeman said to us.

Jaden looked at me; "Yeah" I responded.

"So Oxcile a yuh Uncle" the policeman said

"We don't really talk to police", I brazenly responded.

We had been brought up quite militantly by my father. England was a very racist place to live, particularly in Leicester at the time and as such my Dad wanted us to be tough kids, capable of looking after ourselves. We were brought up on a diet of Malcolm X, Marcus Garvey, Public Enemy and hip hop and almost anything that was anti-establishment so we were accustomed to lashing - out at police, politicians, government, particularly ours at the time Margaret Thatcher, whom Dad absolutely loathed.

Now, alot of people perhaps would have been shit scared of Wadadli police raiding your house with heavy artillery but not us as youngsters. We'd been groomed for this and so were well prepared; calm, actually quite excited whilst others around us seemed quite intense.

**43**

The policeman smiled at my response to him and simply said "Don't worry yourself man your father is not in any trouble, it's just a random check-up"

After a short while Dad was back with us, Uncle ranted for a while longer "Move u bumbaclart outta mi yard man, leave me in peace nuh, wha di fuck you expect fi find" I remember him saying and many other swear words. The head policeman came back into our bed room and made some sort of speech along the lines of Dad staying out of trouble before finally saying; before addressing us all saying……….

"Welcome to Wadadli"

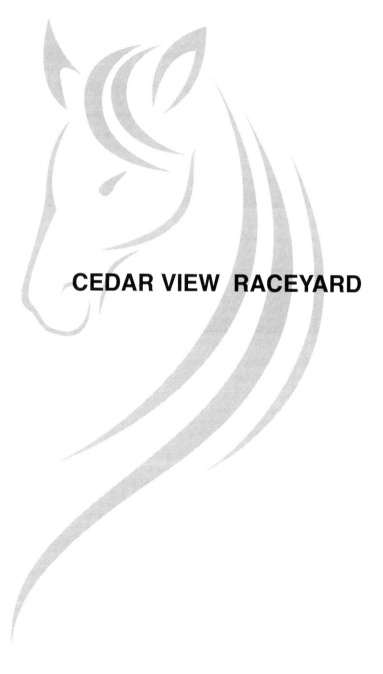

**CEDAR VIEW RACEYARD**

After a few hours of the police leaving, the atmosphere calming down, everybody washed, dressed and fed, uncle stayed true to his word.

"You ready to go see the horse dem?"

"Err yeah sure" I stated.

"Where Jaden deh, come leh we go" Uncle replied back.

Dad was already outside talking to Gully Dawg who was still his animated self even after the police raid. The weather seemed much the same as yesterday, awfully hot and muggy.

I was ready to jump in Uncle's Jeep, but was surprised to find out that we simply had to walk across the main road as the Race Yard was literally just across the road from us! Instantly my thoughts raced back to hearing horses yesterday.

After crossing the road, we had to walk up a slight slope/ hill and then through a gate.

"Welcome to Cedar View Race yard" said Uncle.

I couldn't believe it. I was stunned into excitement. Right before my eyes, horses, stables, paddocks; one of the racehorses a beautiful 'Black Stallion' was being washed outside by one of the workers.

This creature of such stature, I myself had never been afraid of animals, horses or otherwise, but the aura of this animal immediately caught your attention. Its coat was super shiny, so much so that the sun's rays almost reflected off its glossy skin. Pure black with a single white diamond on its forehead and white mark on one of its hind legs just about the hoof, around what you might say would be the equivalent of an ankle. Muscles bulging; so shapely, majestic and strong, veins popping out, tied between two solid posts. He was so handsome.

"That one is Black Silk; we buy him about 2 years ago. He never been beaten in 7 races but he has an injury at the moment so we just getting him back on track slowly; he crazy we have to keep him away from the rest of the animal dem cah he always want to fight".

As Uncle was giving us a breakdown of the horse I noticed all the while it did not take its eyes off us. Jet black eyes they were, for some reason I felt intimidated.

"Freedom and Jaden you all right, you guys get big man, I remember u all from 86. Levi wha you a say, you locks gone man, you decide fi chop dem" the worker said to us whilst washing 'Black Silk'

"This a Chineman, him look Chinese so a dat a wha we call he, he look after the animal dem" Uncle concluded.

I'd by now understood that 'animals' in Antiguan context meant horses; this was part of the lingo. I must agree however that 'Chineman did in fact look Black Chinese!

He was a well-built fella with bad teeth and walked with a limp of some sort. He would in fact become a very good friend of mine.

**47**

The race yard consisted of a huge court yard, 6 enclosed stables for which you had a key to gain access, 2 massive paddocks, a wash area, and a massive copper tub type thing. There were also two stables and a feeding area to the rear. Split between the 6 stables was a large space where the equipment, medication and food were kept. The setup was ever so impressive.

One by one Uncle would introduce us to the racehorses, "this yah a 'Distant Relative', don't go near him he will bite you" this was a brown stallion of medium status with a black mane, at the time he was tied up in his stable and didn't look too amused to see us; as Black Silk was being washed outside, his stable was empty, as was another, "this stable is for 'Star of David' he is a new stallion we buying from Miami he should be coming next week, so we just a left dis yah stable empty for now, so dem a de tree Stallions we have, over here, we have the tree fillies; this one yah is 'Rainbow Melody, she never get beat yet, her father is a very famous horse called Mr Prospector she fast a rass" Uncle proudly chuckled updating us.

She was a gorgeous huge filly, solid and, light brown in hue with a very cute looking white diamond on her forehead and white snip.  At the time she was eating casually with her back to us, occasionally turning around to see who we were and what the fuss was about.

"This is 'Dynamite', she nuh start race yet, she is the sister of Distant Relative, she nah go race until next year,

**48**

but we just keep her in here for now". She was a young small pretty brown mare, with a black mane, similar to her brother really. She came up to us and poked her head over her stable door chewing on some hay, she was very friendly.

"This one is 'Empress Africa', we buy her from America she very fast too but she nah go race much longer we going to breed her wid we stud so we can have some local ponies for the future". Again I'd come to understand that 'ponies' in Antiguan context meant 'foals or baby horses, it was just a Wadadli ting! She was a very elegant looking filly with 4 white socks reaching just above the ankles, a huge white lightening streak marking down her face and grey coat.

Behind this main set of stables was where the Stud was kept; the definition of a stud is a male horse who has the pleasure of doing nothing but breeding female horses in order to produce offspring for racing or whatever purpose.

This thoroughbred was a beast of pure power and was built like the Hulk! However I would find out over time he was in fact one of the most gentle creatures on the yard. Older than me at the time being 15 years of age, he was black with 4 white socks and a white stripe on his face; he was easily the largest horse on the yard. He lived the good life of simply shagging and eating, what more could a fella ask for! His name was 'Cedar View', the Race Yard was named after him.

**49**

It really did surprise me that Uncle actually did have all these animals and the fact they were indeed no ordinary horses but thoroughbreds, racehorses. It was for me the stuff of dreams! It was quite funny to see my dad's reaction as though not scared of the horses he wasn't actually keen on them either.

"So wha happen to 'Monster Mike' it dead? "Dad asked after seeing all the horses in the main setting.

"No no we did sen him to a man in Barbados, he wasn't doing so well after an injury and so we decide fi sell him on, he was a gelding so he couldn't really serve no purpose". Gelding meant 'Monster Mike' had been castrated and so could not have kids.

# THE PROCESSION

Back outside the stables on the courtyard I could see that behind Uncles equestrian setup was a vast expanse of uphill open field stretching for miles, it looked like a dry desert with pockets of bush dispersed all over.

"All a dat is called 'Jallands', its open field it don't belong to nobody" we have about another 4 horses out der, the mares and deh foals dem" said Uncle.

Chineman continued "So you guys like horses, you gonna come to the races?"

"I'm going to coming here every day to help out", was my immediate response.

"A wha yah say racehorse a different type of horse you know, dem nuh easy; but the more help the better so feel free. You want to see the baby horse's dem?" said Chineman

"Ok" I responded

"Yeah; ok let me put 'Silk' in him stable and come". Chineman followed up.

With that said he then un-clipped Black Silk from the washing area posts and wrestled him back into his stable, with us at the time wisely advised to take a few steps back.

I was quick to observe the power of the horse in how it strutted alongside Chineman; puffing out its chest, tail raised with arched neck; neighing boldly as if making a statement along the lines of 'I'm boss'; pure strength;

**52**

it was amazing. The amount of disciple and attention Chineman had to have for this short stint from wash area to stable was also something I noticed instantly; I think anybody would have to be honest.

With Silk in his stable, Chineman would go get a tin container and fill it with horse food pellets before returning to us on the courtyard.

"Watch this" I remember him saying in anticipation.

He began shaking the tin of food, whilst shouting repeatedly 'Come Come Come Come'; 'Come Come Come Come, again and again shaking the pan of food pellets; all the while looking out behind the stables over Jallands.

After a few minutes of this repetitive action he stopped gazing over the barren distance for a few minutes before turning to us.

"You see over deh so" I remember him saying pointing over Jallands.

"To the east, to the east, you see de dust over dere?"

It took a while to understand exactly what it was he was saying and what he wanted us to see; you see in Wadadli they don't say stuff like us in relation to direction. Whilst us here in the UK use descriptive language such as 'to the left or to the right'; Wadadlians say 'to the east or to the west'; yep, making things more than complicated.

Eventually we did get to see what he wanted us to visualize and personally it was one of the most beautiful things.

A small dust cloud at the top of Jallands, probably about 2 – 3 miles from where we were started to appear to snake its way down through the vast expanse seemingly in our direction.

"Come Come Come Come'; 'Come Come Come Come' again and again shaking the pan of food pellets" before pausing for a while awaiting the dust cloud to get ever closer.

This procession of dust would get bigger and bigger as it got closer and closer blitzing towards us, when close enough you could make out that the dust cloud was in fact a 'Herd of Horses' literally racing towards the sound of the tin pan; us!

When about a mile from us, a massive cacophony of sound; galloping hoofs, outlandish neighing, whilst the ground literally shook beneath us was apparent. I remember my dad gripping Jaden whilst looking nervously at me and even Uncle not knowing whether to stand there or flee, it was so wild.

About 100 meters before they reached us I remember Chineman saying to us quite firmly, "just keep a cool head"; his reassurance that everything would be ok we just needed to stay calm.

It was all over in say 3 -4 minutes. We were now surrounded by a carnival of horses 16 in total, 5 of which belonged to Uncle.

# SCHOOL DAYZ

I always felt that Dad made a wrong move taking me out of school in my last year to emigrate and as such apart from the wildlife, racehorses and family; early days, I didn't like much.

School wasn't going to be my favourite place, particularly because you had to wear a uniform and the fact I had a set of friends in the UK whom I was forced to leave; having to start this process all over again seemed like a daunting task.

The school I went to in the UK didn't have uniform and though they wanted to introduce it, we were quite unruly students who resisted it before it finally did become policy a few years later. Khaki chino's and white shirt; black chino's and white shirt on a Wednesday, oh my God, I looked like such a douche I used to think to myself. Me and ma brother made such a fuss about having to wear this stuff that just to appease us Uncle Oxcile brought us the Nike's of our choice. Jaden went for the high top Mowab's and I had the Air Icarus; smiles.

I got into a few arguments with the teachers early days, I remember having to have my parents called in because I use to resist taking off my baseball cap; I refused to sing the national anthem which they did every morning in assembly and I smile today reflecting on when my Dad was called in due to me refusing to speak proper english and just being absolutely rude. Our head teacher couldn't understand why we wanted to speak like them when we already spoke what she would deem the 'Queen Mother's English'!

Due to being new and english we were very popular kids at 'Seatons High'; word also got around the island extremely quickly that we were the nephews of Uncle Oxcile and so all the cool kids wanted to chill with us and all the girls wanted to know us. I remember this one girl who at the time I thought was so hideous constantly asking me in those early days 'Do you have a girlfriend', she had the biggest eyes and the biggest gap between her front teeth I had ever seen, it was so embarrassing. The funny thing is a few years later she actually grew into a fine looking young lady whom all the guys would chase but by that time much to my annoyance she wasn't interested in me!!

Everybody thought that because we were english that we would be good at sport! Luckily me and Jaden were both really good at athletics and ok at basketball. I stated I had always been a particularly gifted kid when it came to track and field, both long distance and short; when it came to 100meters, 800meters or 200 meters I'd only ever lost one race, whilst playing basketball with my peers in Antigua took our game to another level.

Me being me I thought I was good at everything; I remember the PE coach asking if I was any good at football.

'You can play footbawl?' he would ask me.

'Of course' I would reply knowing quite well I was shit.

I remember the Seaton's school team needed players for an upcoming game and how my fellow students had told the coach how fast I was, despite them never seeing me actually play footie.

After a training session where we had to jog a long distance and me coming first in it I was immediately thrown into the first team on game day.

It was so embarrassing how ridiculously rubbish I was; I simply didn't understand the offside rule, the only thing I did of any significance that game was run the length of the pitch on the one occasion I was on –side and win a penalty which our captain scored allowing us to draw the game. It would be my first and last game for 'Seaton's High'!

Once settled what I did like about school was the difference in lessons. Agricultural Science which was for the most part a double practical lesson was fantastic and History was our story. We would cover topics such as the 'Haitian Revolution, study heroes such as Toussaint L'Ouverture, the Maroons of Jamaica, amongst other relevant topics fascinating to me, topics which were only touched upon in England through our parents or during Black History season were now compulsory, key focus subjects.

School had a very disciplined structured and I would be dumbfounded to see young people on many occasions get lashed with belts, rulers for sometimes what I would perceive to be simple things, for example not being in class on time or not having your hair combed! It seemed Mr Jenkins wasn't joking after all! The school catered to students from mostly the surrounding villages but still students would come from afar.

My best friends came from all over and included Devlin also known as 'Butt Tongue', Phathead, Corwin, Kumba, Phatman, Shanty who had a habit of calling me 'Zamplacadoius' and Marvin amongst others, most of whom I'm still in touch with today.

16 04 1994

It's strange reflecting because I know that it did indeed take a while before I would say I was settled in Wadali culture; though Jaden was slightly younger than me I personally believe he settled a lot quicker. A significant turning point for me however was my first birthday in this new land and the five days that followed.

My birthday was on the 16th April it  was 1994 in relation to this recollection and to make things even more crazy, 'today' as I write this chapter, is the 21st April 2015, marking 20 years since what I'm about to share with you actually happened!!

Being as we'd just moved to Wadadli I didn't know what to expect for my birthday. By this time my mother Zulaikah and sister Hawa had joined us, as had been planned as did all our stuff, the horse trailer dad imported and I almost forgot; Dad's bruck up rust bucket of a Land Rover! Dad was like this you see he loved these things!

Though I didn't know what to expect; the last thing that I expected was for my Dad to say 'Freedom me go tek you to de test match, watch cricket'.

I was literally stunned to silence; back in Leicester, England, there was nothing I hated more than going to 'Grace Road' with Jaden and dad to watch boring fucking cricket!! Usually it would be raining, cold and just so dead, for us kids especially.

We hated it with a passion, particularly because when we were even younger Dad would come back from work, walk into the lounge where we were watching 'Teenage Mutant Ninja Turtles' and simply say 'I want to watch the Cricket'; so therefore switch over the tv!! Back in them days even in England, it wasn't like today, we only had the one tv, so obviously this was a violation!!

So that was it off to Antigua's Recreation Ground we went in the Land Rover to watch West Indies vs England, man how I was hiding in the back of that ting all the way!!

Antigua is a small island smaller than the whole of Leicestershire. You could drive around the whole island in one day, howere it has many smaller islands off of it and as mentioned its twin Barbuda.

It didn't take long to get to the 'Recreation Ground', a matter of minutes, one straight road one set of traffic lights heading east from the village to the town centre.

The atmosphere surprised me as we got to the town centre, it was more like a fringing carnival than cricket me and Jaden thought to ourselves.

It was electric, people all colourful, dressed up, proud to represent the island and team. Happy chanting, the enchanting smell of jerk chicken cooking, soca music blasting, and whistles, a lot of whistles going off and this was all outside the Recreation Ground, this was us just pulling up!

So many people, all of us flocking to this 'Ground'

'WE GO SEN DEM RASS BACK A ENGLAND!'

'BOMBACLART DEM GO GET SOME LICKS EH!'

'YEAH MAN, DEM CYAN COME A DADLI COME FUCK AROUND, WE GO KILL DE ENGLISH MAN DEM LORD GAD!'

'GIMME TWO GUINESS'

These were common themes in the conversations of the people around us as we jammed to the stadium.

**61**

**LARA**

As stated in the previous chapter, the events over the next 5 days truly allowed me to embrace the fact that Antigua was now home.

Still pissed due to having to attend a cricket match on my birthday but now intrigued due to the magnitude of the difference in atmosphere here in Antigua, it was a rude awakening having actually entered the 'Recreation Ground'.

It's difficult to put into words how special this event was. The first observation was that the last thing you thought, after witnessing events was that a cricket match was about to commence! Well for me anyway!

Amongst the crush; young people galore; Soooo many pretty girls, many of whom I'd recognised from school but now looking lovely out of uniform, others whom I didn't know just looking gorgeous, sound systems booming, people dancing merrily, others chilling merrily but everybody joyous full of cheer and laughter. It was mesmerising, almost hypnotic not to love the vibe and although there were police patrolling, even they joined in the occasion and were in good spirit generally.

Everywhere you turned you would see beer stands selling Carib beers, Wadadli beers, Guinness, Red Stripe, Super malts; I remember this dude who was dressed real strange high on a platform dancing real crazy; headgear, stockings, crop top luminous colours as well, what was going on, I later found out his name was Gravy, the good luck mascot and this was how he carried on every test match.

So much food on sale; roast corn, roasted peanuts, all these flavours engulfing the air and blended with the smell of Barbecue Chick, which was served with bread; ice cream, soft drinks like Ting, Coca Cola, Vimto for those who didn't drink, you're talking thousands of people.

Dad would pick up goodies for us all, we then had to make our way to 'Bleachers Stand' named so due to the area having no cover to protect you from the sun; this is where all Dads friends and many of our family were situated.

Dad would be so 'in his element', once settled, he would leave us to wander with our friends to explore, so it was a case of constantly looking over our shoulder to make sure Hawa was ok being that she was the youngest and tagging along with us.

We had by now got to know quite well many of our young family members, had made quite a few friends and Antigua was a place where everybody knew everybody so you could never get lost despite the thousands of people present, it felt ever so comfortable.

There was something for everybody to do, I'd come to realise that even those who were not into cricket would be here just for the fun vibes.

When we got exhausted from the heat and wandering chasing girls we would head back to dad to chill out and watch the game; It was like an education particularly for the first few days of getting to understand the rules of the game and meeting people/ family all in this one place.

By the third day it was evident that something special was taking place here. The West Indies were thrashing England and one player in particular was doing extremely well, his name was Brian Lara.

"LARA! LARA! BWOY HIM A GWAN BAD U KNOW!!"

"DROP SOME BAT PON DEM RASS"

"SEN DEM RASS BACK A ENGLAND LARA"

This would be Dad amongst others excited by how this young man from Trinidad was playing.

I was now understanding the game much better and starting to join in the excitement regards how well game was panning out. As England were losing it seemed as if my allegiance was slowly switching from feeling English to feeling Caribbean. I would never say Antiguan because I was always aware I was dual heritage and part Jamaican through my mother which I was also extremely proud of and very different to Antiguan in Culture.

# 375 THE REST IS HISTORY

England were looking absolutely bemused; this guy was making Angus Fraser, Chris Lewis and the others look like muppets; a Century, a double century and now 300 runs on the last day and still not out? Brian Lara was on the verge of history!

Angus Fraser going through his preparations before running up and bowling, flinging the ball all types of ways; BLUKKU!!! The sound of the ball being smacked by Lara sending it raining down on the crowd for another 6; same for Chris Lewis BLATOW!!! His ball getting smashed high into the heavens out the ground for another 6. The joke was that some of the balls must have been ending up in the prison yard which was situated outside the 'Recreation Ground' to the east of it.

The stand on the final day where we were based was now ram with people who weren't necessarily based here on the first few days, but this was how it went, people would float about in the stadium and end up wherever. It was quite funny because I had now come to understand that what Jah Bless was smoking that first day we landed was in fact Marijuana better known as Ganja over here and most people situated where we were, was smoking it. It got so bad that somebody snitched and so we now had for the last 2 days a policeman patrol our stand quite observantly, but still very lenient due to him himself not wanting to miss the match. No arrests were made as far as I remember.

**67**

"BWOY MI HERE THE ISLAND EMPTY TO RASSCLAART"

"HIM GO BROKE DE RECORD YOU KNOW"

People were crying with laughter at the prospect of 'Sir Garfield Sobers' world record being broken right here in front of us on Antiguan soil.

The tension, the excitement, the banter, the cheer, at every ball blasted into the stratosphere was crazy crazy crazy and even the defensive play. These Wadadlians were going looney and me, Hawa and Jaden couldn't help but join in. Half of Antigua's population must have been in the stadium this day as it was absolutely saturated with people, more than previous days.

'BLUKKU' another 4, BLATOW another 6, PLIE!!!! The look of defeat was well written on the faces of the English, Phil Tuffnell, Mark Ramperkash, all of them, well beaten, nothing could stop this supreme being in his element.

Mid-afternoon; Brain Lara was now astonishingly 20 runs from breaking Sir Garfield Sobers world record which had stood for 36 years, something not even the Great Vivian Richards could achieve, how was this even happening.

"YOU SEE SOBERS OVER DEH, LORD GOD, HIM RECORD GONE HAHAHA, LARA LARA!!" Dad would chant.

Well before this point people were beginning to get more animated and you could tell that 'if' this dude was to break 'Sir Garfield Sobers' record, it would kick off mad scenes of jubilation.

The police recognised this and began to put into operation some form of security by making a ring around the edge of the pitch. They had decided to draft in extra officers for potential events of over excitement should the day prove to be historical.

"Officer you nah stop I and I you know, you better call in the whole of the force and di army fi stop we you know boss"; people were happily declaring their intentions, and the officers themselves, though excited, looked confused in relation to how they were going to adequately pull off whatever they were planning.

I can't really remember in my lifetime many more emotional moments than this day.

England were by now well and truly beaten and with approximately 10 runs left all the music in the stadium was stopped with only the 'crazy looking man, Gravy' wearing his colourful head gear and luminous cycling shorts' high up on his own platform playing 'The Last Post' blowing from a horn much to the amusement of all in the stadium; over and over he would blow this tune from his horn.

BLUKKU 6 runs left, the tension was unreal, POW 3 runs left tension now unbearable and finally!

Chris Lewis ran up after his familiar routine, flung the ball; 'BLATOOOWWWW!!!!!!' and a cheer which I'm sure triggered a mini earthquake! The world record was smashed into oblivion.

The jubilant young man, arms wide open as if inviting all to celebrate with him, looking to the heavens with a massive smile on his face. The crowd bursting into celebration invading the pitch, the police not knowing what to do trying to grab this person and the next, then letting him go and trying to grab her, then just becoming utterly overwhelmed, letting everybody go whom they had caught and themselves joining in the fun whilst still trying to protect the player and players from over eager fans.

We had witnessed a moment of genius, history, 375 declared; I had now fallen in love with cricket, fallen in love with Antigua.

# JAMTIGUAN MUSLIMS

So yeah; Mum and sis had by now joined us and as a result me, Jaden and Hawa had to move out of the family house to our Aunt's. We still however spent all our time at Uncle's and it was more a case of just sleeping at Aunties which was closer to our school, more or less across a football pitch across the village.

Mum was the religious head of our family, she was the gentle and caring, the parent who helped with the homework and practically did all the childcare stuff, and she was fun and understanding, the parent you would share your problems with.

Mum came from a strong Jamaican family called the 'Wints' proud of the fact our great uncle was 'Arthur Wint' who was the first Jamaican athlete to bring back a gold medal to Jamaica; we would always hear this story amongst our Jamaican family elders!

The fact mum was Jamaican also meant that for her this was going to be a new experience too; I didn't clock at first but after a while could see that she wasn't as comfortable as maybe us kids thought, I mean she went from having all her immediate family around her to not having any at all and like I said previously; though both islands, Antigua and Jamaica were in the Caribbean, they had their own characteristics culturally, socially, and economically.

When mum and dad got together they went through many religious phases, mum was Christian before she met dad, then became Rastafarian after meeting Dad, then a year before I was born they reverted to Islam though kept our Rastafarian culture.

Though it was my Dad who made the first steps to embracing Islam; by the time we had got to Antigua Dad wasn't really a practising Muslim, it was our mother and my aunty from mums side who also embraced Islam when mum and dad did, who taught us almost everything regards being muslim and they taught us well.

By the time I was 12 I could recite my prayers fluently in Arabic and could take on anybody really, debate wise, when it came to religious topics. I give dad credit for teaching us about the Malcolm X's, Marcus Garvey's, Che Guevara's, Nelson Mandela's; Dad was the more revolutionary minded parent of the family.

Dad did in fact have 5 other children with different women, but for mum, it was me, Jaden and Hawa. Hawa was the baby of us three; as she was a girl and the youngest, Dad was very protective of her and as such she wasn't allowed the freedom of movement, me and Jaden had and often was stuck with Mum doing women things I guess. She was a cool sister though; the three of us grew up really tight.

**73**

So settling into life in the early days in Wadadli our daily routine would involve school, then straight off to the stables to help out, back to Uncles across the road to clean up and eat, playing streetfighter on the Nintendo with our cousins 'Che and O'shae and Junior', kissing Mum about 8pm before bouncing off to the other side of the village to our Aunt's to sleep.

During these days which you could call the honeymoon period, often Uncle would take us and his children to the fancy parts of the island like English Harbour for pizzas and so on, there were days where mum and dad would also take us to the beach, they were fun times. We were really getting to know one another familywise and ironically losing our English accents all at the same time.

# HORSEBWOY

Life over at the stables for the first year was quite basic. I was there more or less every single day due to my passion for the animals. Jaden was there just as much but just not as much as me.

I'd got to understand the working routine of grooming, feeding, washing when necessary, I'd come to understand when the racers needed  re – shoeing, the difference in management for the stud, and when the brood mares and foals needed rounding back to base from out at pasture for checks ups.

I was very observant and although I wasn't allowed to do too much in the first year regard training the horses, I was quickly up to speed regarding how that went too.

I'd got to know the chief trainer whose nickname was 'Bullet', he was around Uncle's age and him and Uncle went way back, I didn't know his real name. He seemed quite a smug dude, didn't tend to say much to me and Jaden. I'd also got familiar with the jockeys who would come to ride the horses out or I'd meet them down at the race track weeks before a race, in preparation for a race day.

The training leading up to a race day was truly something to behold. Being that we now had 2 horse trailers we were able to double the number of animals we could transport around.

One of the key methods of training I particularly loved was when we took the animals to the beach; I would watch 'Bullet' and 'Chineman' swim the racehorses way out to sea sometimes a mile out and lunge the animals out there in the middle of the magical Caribbean ocean oblivious to the very real danger of Tiger Sharks and obvious health and safety risks as this would all be done with just a simple head collar and lead chain nothing more.

English and American tourists would stop to take pictures, astonished, stunned at the level of danger, skill and beauty of animal, man and scenery on these occasions.

Swimming was a very good form of exercise for the horses in that it allowed every muscle in the animals body to be worked. It was also very useful for the animals that had cuts, bruises, and injuries of the leg due to not having to put weight on the legs whilst the healing properties of the sea were local knowledge to the Islanders.

We had training jockeys and race day jockeys; our training jockeys would ride out on the racers on many different selected routes equivalent to bridleways in preparation for race day and the distance route agreed by 'Bullet' would always be determined by the number of days till race day, the race the horse was to feature in, its level of fitness and the horse itself relative to all of this.

As stated the 'Don' had a few houses and the beach we tended to use was not too far from his main house, as a result, we would often pass by for a few minutes, so as to update him on the horses training progress; sometimes you wouldn't see him for days on end, he was a hard man to pin down at the best of times, so this was a good way of linking up with him.

If you pictured the 'Family yard' back in the village being nice you should have seen this yard. OMG, the bungalow was soooo impressive. Made of all masonry, some parts marble. The yard had its own private road that filtered off the main road round the back of the yard in a semi circle layout; an absolutely massive satellite dish probably about as big as a double decker bus, whilst surrounded by a huge garden encased by a circular fence. The lawn was always immaculate and the yard was posted out with a few of 'The Dons' henchmen, I'd come to know them as.

It was rumoured Uncle had about 30 children for about 15 women back in 1995 at the time of print I'm not sure what that figure is; one of his elder children 'Raggamuffin, Marlon' lived at this yard. He was a young man of few words, a Rasta yout, Jah Bless's full brother but the total opposite; he had a well-known sound system that was doing real well at the time called 'Crucifix'. Raggamuffin was into Pitbulls and I'd come to learn that Gringo back at the village family yard belonged to him; he had another here at this yard a black and white female called 'Carrie', she was a lovely looking bitch.

**WINNERS**

I'd never been to the races in the UK, it's not something you would associate the black minority ethnic communities of the inner cities where Caribbean folk mostly lived.

So though extremely excited to witness my first actual race day' I didn't know what to expect, but I'll tell you now it was truly something to behold.

So we get up early like 05:30am; it's strange because the horses are acting like they know its race day. It was like they been through the routine that many times that they recognised the signs/ see certain things leading up to race day and put two and two together. Believe me do not underestimate horses they are extremely intelligent creatures.

For my first race day we had just the one racer, Distant Relative and the distance he was due to run was 6 furlongs which meant the distance, this was a fairly short distance more of a sprint race. As a result I was able to observe the surroundings and what was about to occur. The 'Antiguan Turf Club' in Cassada Gardens this was where the Race Track was based and it was managed by the Turf Club. Upon first observations everywhere just looked run down; the race track didn't look like much; it was more the people and surroundings that made it what it was.

Our routine would be, unloading the Distant Relative from the trailer where Chineman would then take him to his stable. Again as if making a statement Distant Relative would neigh boldly so as to signal to every other horse present at the racetrack his arrival.

"Wha a gwan mi bredrin" an old Rastafarian leading one of our rival racers past us said.

"You all ready for some licks today yah?" he would cheekily conclude with banter flying back the other way from our contingent.

Horse racing is taken extremely seriously, for some reason we always had to have somebody posted outside Distant Relative's stable if we happen to have other horses racing then somebody would have to be posted outside each stable sometimes 2 people to outside a stable depending on the race and horse involved. This was because horse racing was big money and a lot of it depended on strategy though many a time fights and arguments would break out due to what many would perceive as bribery, cheating.

The smell of Avocado and Salt fish baguettes so pungent; everybody in their best cloths; and the music; dancehall music blaring out from sound systems made the atmosphere absolutely amazing. As amazing as it was what really interested me were the animals. I would venture through the race yard which was separated from the racetrack to observe the many different racers from all over the island. Each animal from the varying stables had their own colours and though everybody was more or less friendly with each other, there was an intense rivalry which was acutely evident amongst our stable peers.

Thirty or so minutes before Distant Relative's race, we would have to prepare him in his race colours, Black and Gold, his racing saddle and bandages. Racing gear was solely for race day, special attention is given to the animals on this day as this is the day others would see your horse, its condition and so on, so you always would want to make an impression and highlight your brand through the horse's presentation.

Once the race would start the music would stop and everybody would flood to the stands to respect the race. Some people would be on the roofs of stables, whilst for those who did not have a horse racing in a particular race would still be stationery outside their racers stable as if standing guard; for sure during a race is when you needed to be most cautious with regards to things going wrong.

Nothing beats race day in Wadadli, it would become the day I would most look forward to for many reasons. Regards Distant Relative's race during my first race day, he came second to whom I would later find out was his arch rival 'Tax Angel'.

# SIMMER DOWN

If the first year spent in Antigua was all about settling in, then the second was about 'the transition'. The transition from merely being a newbie to feeling accepted and understanding who we were in terms of a family and how it was structured and operated.

We'd come to understand that Uncle Oxcile was one of the most notorious drug dealers on the island. He had his fair share of fans and haters; there were those who loved him, those who disliked him, those who despised him but everybody respected him and almost all feared him, and for good reason.

This was a man who had been deported from the United States for his criminal activities and was also banned from the UK. It's fair to say though that to us family members, he was nothing more than a business man and a family man who looked after all his immediate family, his extended family and all friends and associates, that included his 30 or so kids he was legendarily known for. These included a few in the United States, most in Antigua and God knows wherever else! People said he had a kid in China! Whether it was true or not, I really couldn't tell you.

By the end of the year we were dominating the race scene with our horses with me and Jaden now fully integrated members of the race yard; both grooms. We had more or less the same friends as the gap in age between us was only 18 months. Basketball became a key social activity for us and we would often hit the ball

**84**

court after our stable duties and dinner around 7pm, sometimes staying as late as 11pm – 12pm. It didn't matter that we were 15 going on 16 and 14 respectively because we had to always get up early in tune with everybody else, plus the sun would be roasting from morning making it impossible to sleep beyond morning anyway.

Dad by now had just started a farm and had a few goats and sheep. He had decided that we were going to have our own butchers and so the farm became an extension of the race yard.

Dad by now had also become one of Uncles most trusted workers of his 'Inner cirlce' regarding other activities and as such we started to understand more and more 'how things went'.

The Don was the head of an empire and as such had his fingers in many pies; he had many assets. He had the Jeep, the Porsche, Acura Legend, Suzuki Jeep, Saab, Lexus, and say another 3 or 4 cars I can't remember, he had a JCB, a horse trailer, the stables, a huge speed boat, a massive truck, 3 houses that I knew of, the beauticians and many other things I just can't remember. He did have at one point a petrol station which he shared with my aunty but things went sour with that and as such he kind of lost it to her.

Over time I'd understood that Uncle identified more with a certain type of audience as did Aunty. Aunty was truly religious as was Gran and you could never spend an hour in eithers presence without them mentioning how Jesus Christ was the 'Son of God' and so on.

Uncle, despite being a notorious drug baron, was also surprisingly religious and went to church every Sunday whenever he could. This was probably one of the few places you could guarantee finding him. However outside of Church his associates were nearly all members of the criminal underworld and those who weren't were usually paid through some sort of criminal activity or favour.

The biggest commodity to 'The Don's' empire however was the control he had regarding the islands drugs monopoly.

# WEED BY THE POUND

14 months on and Uncles horses were dominating the race scene, we were playing serious ball on the ball court with our friends, were now comfortable hitting the city centre with friends or by ourselves and we were now involved in 'local donkey races'!!

Yeah donkey races!! They were quite competitive too and earned us a few dollars to be honest; race days for the donkeys would be every Saturday.  Between me and Jaden we had 3 donkeys 'Queen Latifah, Sheba and Mega Man'. Donkeys are a common feature and valuable asset in Antigua not only for young people but adults alike. We would create our own race tracks and had a few spotted across the outskirts of the village.

Donkey racing didn't last long for me however; I was getting lanky now and didn't think personally that riding a donkey was for me. So I focused more on training the animals, with me and Jaden often injecting the animals with the race horses vitamins for example B12, keeping them in stables and feeding them quality horse food and tonic aiming for that competitive edge which we ultimately had. Basically imitating the racehorses regime.

Our time from here on in was far from fun and games however. Dad and Uncle were closer than Dad and Aunty and as such we kind of pledged alleigence to 'The Don' which brought its own benefits and setbacks to all associated with him.

I remember the first big move we made and the complex nature of our life now.

It must have been like 2am or 3am in the morning.

"Freedom, Jaden come let we go" said Dad.

What was going on? Dad was whispering, seemed real animated but excited and why on earth was he waking us up at ridiculous hour in the morning?

"Get on your tings we have fi mek a move, don't turn on the light, see ur tings dem yah" Dad said.

"Where we going?" I asked whilst Jaden was still stirring getting himself together.

"Nuh bother wid de questions dem just get ur tings dem on and come let we go" Dad instructed

"Ok" I responded.

Whatever it was we were going to do it seemed real important. I mean to have Dad on edge the way it did it must have been.

Once up we followed Dad out the house in peer darkness and had to follow him over to the race yard where we were greeted by about 8 of Uncle's inner circle, some family, some friends.

Gully Dawg, Chineman, Raggamuffin, Jah Bless, Mookie, Irvine, Cashew Nut and of course the Don; Uncle

"Everybody ok' Uncle said as we all circled around him.

"Yeah man" everybody would mumble one way or another.

**89**

"We have a shipment coming through any minute, Colombian, 8 tonne, my man set up everyting".

You see we had over at the stables a secret location where we were able to store tonnes of marijuana which would come to the island transported by boat from all over the Caribbean; sometimes Jamaica, sometimes Trinidad, St Vincent, this particular load was coming from Columbia. So this move was a case of stashing the new shipment which took roughly 2 hours to complete.

Minibus after minibus would come to the race yard to dispatch a load. Huge bundles of compressed tightly wrapped marijuana. Once it arrives 4 guys would be responsible for unloading, 2 would bust down the outer packaging whilst another 3 would stack, leaving 2 guys to look out.

It was a supremely organised operation; where all these minibuses came from I'll never know. I didn't know the drivers either but by then everybody knew their responsibilities and positions. Me and Jaden's position was to help with the stacking. Man the amount of herb we were dealing with Snoop Dogg would have been in heaven!

5kg slabs, 15kg slabs, 20kg slabs one after the other neatly sealed as if professionally; for young people our age it was hard work but with everybody working together the time would pass by quite quickly. During this time the focus was extremely intense, limited talking and ultimate teamwork. It was said Uncle had police working for him too and they would assist in the operations to ensure it played out smoothly.

As soon as everything was unloaded, there would be a lot of fist bump action, we would lock up the race yard, everybody would go they separate ways disappearing into the night. This routine became the norm moving forward and would be carried out on a regular frequent basis.

You see I could understand why Dad never had a problem with engaging us in this activity. Coming from Rasta himself, Dad never ever had a problem with marijuana, getting older we had come to know the difference between tobacco and ganja, and I guess he trusted us more, whilst with this being our new environment I guess to him made it more acceptable. It didn't faze me that I was 15 years old and Jaden a year younger; I guess it was just family business.

# EMBRACING RASTA

Nobody needed to tell us that we had to remain tight lipped regards our night time movements assisting Uncle. As time went by it became very apparent that we were the family that ran tings on this island.

In the village me and Jaden got a lot of respect; in the horse world we were now well known and at school we were well integrated; cool guys.

Mum wasn't getting on very well regards adapting to Wadadli culture, she was Jamaican and so it was understandable. She had accepted a job with my aunt Cassie who ran a college but was having issues with her personally and apparently Aunty wasn't paying mum properly at the time much to mums annoyance.

Me and Jaden as well as Hawa were becoming increasingly close to Jah Bless and his crew of friends who were all Rastafarians. The only Muslim we knew who existed on the island apart from us, was my Dad's friend Musa Heskey who also spent many of his years in England where a lot of his family were based; but he was dads age and lived on the other side of the island so we didn't have any real connection with him from a youngsters perspective.

As a family we also were not practicing, which made mum feel even more uncomfortable. She would try her best, but she was not supported by my father whose favourite drink was now Guinness and it seemed as if they were somehow growing apart. Though a loving father I found him very disrespectful to my mother often resorting to domestic violence as if to somehow get some kind of point across, the affect this had on us he would come to find out later.

I think as a result of all of this Jah Bless became somewhat of a protective figure in our eyes. You see being Muslim we couldn't identify with aunty and grandma's Christian teachings; but the more time we spent around Jah Bless the more his Rastafarian teachings seemed ever so similar to Islam in many ways; cultural ways.

He had a good friend in the village by the name of 'Julian' who was an elder Rasta; he would let Jah Bless and his crew use his small house as a type of preparation base away from the yard. Jah Bless was interested in one thing and one thing only ……. Herb. He smoked a lot of weed, he was a proper Rasta, but a cool Rasta, he would say he was on the 'Highest Meditation'; always.

Smoking ganja, selling ganja and reading scripture whilst playing his role as a family member was really his daily routine. He would from time to time disappear to the United States to where he grew up; sometimes for 2 months, 3 months and so forth so we always found it a real pleasure to be around him when he was here. The fact he was into his hip hop a little, dressed like a hip hop kid and had this American accent made his aura extra appealing too. He was genuinely just a pleasant dude.

At first we would hang out around him and his crew asking questions and just watching what they did; cleaning weed, which involved a key or 2 of compressed ganja, chopping it, removing buds off the stems and then de-seeding it and bagging it up; all whilst smoking it; not us, them at this point.

He would ask us about how we see Islam and explain Rastafari to us, allowing us to see the books he would read for example the 'Kebra Negast', who His Imperial Majesty King Haile Selassie I was to him and how Ganja was a blessed plant because it was found on His Imperial Majesty King Haile Selassie grave and opened up 'your third eye'. Other occasions we would go with him to his secret Ganja Farm where he had huge crops of Wadadli Ganja growing.

He would ask us many questions about religion, spirituality; and many a time his crew would be cooking the most delicious pots of Ital food! Pure vegetarian meals, delicately and deliciously prepared. Jah Bless was one of the truest Rastafarians I'd come to know and his influence was growing daily.

**HURRICANE LUIS**

"Hurricane a come nuh"; Chinks sounded unsure, asking a rhetorical question as if talking to himself.

"Bwoy so dem a sey" Irvine responded.

"Tomorrow me here, superstorm dem sey nuh, me here it go bad bad bad" Chinks followed up, with Jah Bless being the head of this group of men, deciding to end the conversation with "Salassie I watch over I n I you know star, whats to be will be, Jah knows best".

This was the chat at Julian's yard, the yard all of Jah Bless's crew chilled at; it must have been about 2pm in the afternoon September 3 1995 and everybody but me, Jaden, Hawa and obviously Jah Bless seemed real nervous.

Things were going real well; the animals were literally paying for themselves with the earnings from the races they were winning. 'Rainbow Melody' had just won the Filly Classic and 'Star of David' had won the Heineken Cup whilst Distant Relative' came first in his race too, so up until this week everything was bless.

You see in Wadadli there are two seasons, dry season; and hurricane season, and it was Hurricane season in a big way. During this season islanders pay attention to the weather bulletins intensely and it had been announced last week that a 'Category 4' storm was heading directly towards us. Category 4 meant 'Super storm'.

Antigua had already been relatively stormy due to the season and we had been relatively blessed in terms of being able to avoid the storms unlike many of the islands about us such as Montserrat which had the added threat of the Soufriere Hills Volcano eruption, Martinique, Guadeloupe and Trinidad; however that was all about to change.

I remember the day before the storm nobody was in a jokey mood at all, well none of our friends anyway. Everybody stuck to their families and everybody except me, brother and sister seemed to have something to do; this was new to us so we just sat back and observed.

For the last few days people were buying out the shops, boarding up windows and reinforcing doors, letting out animals, the vulnerable would be packing things ready to be collected by relatives moving to theirs until the storm was to pass, or seeking shelter at our school, which had been converted into an emergency shelter for anybody who felt at risk in there homes; it was crazy, but not for us, for us this was exciting.

"Bwoy it go mad, what time you think it go hit?"

"Me cyan wait bwoy, what it like really, me hear Rastaman all a fly tru dem air cah dem so light a tru, wha mek everybody a gwan so fraid; a so bad it be for real".

These would be the kind of things we would be saying.

"Bwoy unnuh hafi come from England, unnuh crazy no fuck".

"Hurricane kill people you know, a wha de tall yah, you guys are directly crazy".

That would generally be my friend's answers to our boisterous chants of excitement and humorous piss taking chuckles.

I remember being in our house, mid – afternoon, which due to the boarding up of the windows and reinforcing of the doors, was really dark and haunting, and even more so as it got late. Late afternoon people were still outside doing whatever little things they could. A lot of water was stacked by families, emergency stuff like batteries, torches, matches little things like these. During this time you could feel a strange light breeze which kept you conscious of some type of 'happening' heading our way.

Over across the stables everything was secure, the animals were well fed. The building was solid, structured in such a way we didn't envisage too many problems despite this being a Super storm and anyway no matter how much you prepare in this type of a situation 'what was to be, would be' as we were constantly reminded. In fact the stables were more secure than many people's houses and we could see the stables from the house through the front door glass panes which were so small they didn't really need to be boarded up.

**99**

As it got late it was noticeable how the winds had picked up and by now everybody was indoors. It must have been around 9pm yet it was getting extremely dark, you could just about figure out certain images depending on which window gaps you found to peep from. The banging and clattering was eerily constant; within a few minutes we could truly now say we were in the midst of a storm.

My expectations were somewhat dampened however as time ticked as I had this vision of seeing like a whirlwind mass of cloud coming to us but it never really panned out that way. I guess that's where watching too many disaster movies back in England comes into play. Even if there was a mass of monstrous cloud, by about 9.30pm it would have been impossible to work out due to how dark it was.

My first moment of feeling uneasy, realising this was serious must have been around 11pm; that's when it sunk in that we were using candles instead of electricity, there was no TV to watch, mum was praying in Arabic becoming increasingly worried and outside, lashing rain unlike anything we had heard, with the wind to give that added effect; at times the wind sounded like a high pitched lady screaming for dear life and at other times like a thousand lions roaring, it was unreal; out there sounded absolutely menacing.

# BIRDS FLY BACKWARDS

I slept relatively easy throughout the night, our house was a solid structure and as such even though there was constant crash, bang, wallop going on, I was more excited than scared so I slept fine.

Us young'uns must have crashed out about 12:00am as it was such an isolated feeling of not having much too do, being able to see much that the excitement kinda turned to bordom. I knew also that in the morning the storm would still be going on in full effect and so wanted to witness as such thus going sleep meant rising to anticipation.

What I woke up to was astonishing!

I remember going to the front door with Jaden and looking out across the stables through the glass pane. Every single telegraph post was either ripped out the ground or lopsided. The roof of the race yard stables was ripped clean off, dangling as if by a piece of thread violently to and fro; one of the horse trailers had been spun around the opposite way whilst the race yard and paddock fencing was heavily destroyed in places. I was thinking to myself if that's the state of the stables how are the horses!

Now there are three specific parts to a hurricane; the beginning, the eye, and tail. The eye of the storm is basically the centre of the storm; it's a very strange period as during this time everything is practically dead calm.

We were waiting for this particular time as we knew we would be able to run across to the stables to check on the horses and that's exactly what we did.

"Come let we go; Freedom; Jaden" dad said.

Outside was surreal, quite, a dead silence, most things were either torn up, lopsided or damaged. Reaching the stables it wasn't good, 'Star of David' was literally standing in water up to his chest, we decided to move him to a stable towards the rear of the main set of stables with 'Cedar View' simply for better protection. Despite what they had been through over the last few hours 'Star of David' was easy going with regards to moving stables.

We didn't have much time to work with during the eye perhaps fifteen to twenty five minutes and as such after basic checks on the animals we simply gave them more food, fresh water and hay. Apart from 'Star of David's stable situation everything else wasn't too bad and being we were half way there now being in the eye of the storm, we only had the tail to deal with.

With the wind picking up we had to eventually head back inside, the tail of the storm was much the same as the beginning just everything was visible. Super strong winds and driving rain, flying galvanise, flying wire, coconuts; birds being forced to fly backwards, yeah it was rough.

With the storm declared over 36 hours later, it was the trail of destruction which would last months that hit us the hardest. We had a generator and so we could function a lot better than most during the aftermath; for a long time the whole island didn't have any electricity, hot water; many roads were blocked due to debris, food was short as was clean water, but this was the same for all islanders. What hit us the hardest was the impact on our business as a family.

Horse Racing was postponed for a long time due to the Race Track being badly damaged, food pellets were hard to come by, there was a shortage of ganja to the island what we would call a drought and as a result this affected funds; lack of funds meant a lack of loyalty.

'Bullet' being the main man in control of the stables had disappeared; as did the training jockeys and a few other essential persons for the stables like the guys who used to cut the grass for the animals; Chineman stayed loyal but during these tough times the horses suffered a lot and had it not been for myself, Dad, Jaden and Chineman going the extra mile without pay, the animals would have suffered even more.

Every single day we had to cut grass with machetes just to feed the horses, something we hadn't previously had to do. This lasted for a good few months until things picked back up again. It was during these times that I learnt how to drive, because of how difficult things were it was important I could drive not only the Landrover but the Landrover with the horse trailer attached which we would fill with grass and take back for the race horses.

During this period we grew a lot as horsemen and I started to have more and more influence over how we did things regarding creating an emergency routine to keep the animals on track. Eventually Jaden would become the chief training jockey, I would become the chief trainer, Dad played his part and tended to look out for Cedar View and Chineman supported everything we did.

Around this time that I had to learn how to swim the racehorses which in my opinion equated to 'swimming with sharks!' It didn't take long to master however and it would be a common occurrence where on training days to the beach I would swim way out to sea with one of the horses attached to a lead rope wearing just a head collar. I conquered my nerves regarding this task by using the time to reflect on good times, the family business, and with the animals depending on us, I wasn't about to let them or our family down.

During these months myself and Jaden became much darker young men in our views, movements and loyalty to Uncle. The Don seen what we did and what we were doing, appreciated it and ultimately gave us a huge amount of control over this particular asset, the race yard whilst also allowing us to run ganja for him and ultimately ourselves.

# THINGZ DON CHANGE

So fast forward 4 months, the island was getting back to normal, me and Jaden now had a half breed Pitbull called Blood that we took off of Raggamuffin, we had also managed to trick Dad into getting a three quarter Pitbull quarter Rottweiler puppy and we were now experimenting with weed. We also sported huge afro's kept neat and tight by a stocking. Uncle was getting some weed to the island but not as much as we were used to and so though things were better on this front it was still relatively slow.

Mum had left to go back to England for something or the other, whilst me and Jaden were still in control of the horses and doing relatively well. Uncle was now paying us on a more regular basis and asking us a lot of questions regards the race horses progress as during the aftermath of the storm, some lost alot of weight and there were naturally alot of other problems.

With me coordinating each training program for each animal; Jaden executing the training and dad being the transporter, we managed to win our first few races back out on track. At first 'Distant Relative' was our only runner due to his fantastic condition since the hurricane and the other horses' poor condition. However he was winning and as such his earnings were virtually running the stables bringing a lot of confidence to all of us involved.

It was around 2 months later that Uncle made a move that changed how I looked at him, us as a family and myself.

I believe Uncle took us for granted; after all our loyalty in virtually rescuing his equestrian empire; he didn't tell us he was planning to bring back 'Bullet'. We now had our own links and therefore had heard this through the grapevine. What made this really sour was that 'Bullet' himself we had come to know, defected to our competitor's stables and so we, those of us who had upheld the stables viewed him as a traitor.

Now anything Uncle did nobody questioned, however me growing as a young man and in stature as a racehorse training weed smoking hustler was not prepared to accept his decision to let this guy swan back to our stables and take over the reins! No way; I remember the day he came back.

I had caught wind whilst at school that 'Bullet' was over at the stables working with the horses, my blood was boiling. I couldn't wait for school to finish and as it did I marched home to change out of my school clothes, with Jaden and a few friends. I remember reaching the yard looking over to the stables and seeing Uncles Jeep, Bullets pick up as well as dad's Land Rover and quite a few people. I was now filled with rage.

How could Uncle allow this guy to come back to work for him? How could he undermine us the way he did? How could he not tell us? Is he expecting us to all be jolly again? How much is he paying this dude? What role will we now play? Do we go back to being grooms? All of these questions running through my mind as me, Jaden and friends' rolled up a couple of spliffs en route Cedar Views race yard.

To this day me and Jaden still talk about what transpired, him always referring to the glaze in my eyes as I walked past all the fake smiles tunnel vision straight to Bullet; all I remember was Bullet with his smug smile standing there waiting to greet me I imagine, dad sitting screw face in his Landrover staring obliviously away from the 'Don's henchmen and the party greeting Bullets apparent return; Uncles gold and diamond teeth glistering; me there yet nobody willing to say anything, now a few feet from Bullet still walking towards him.

And then it happened

'SMACK!!!'

"You a bloodclaart traitor"

I'd launched myself at this guy I deemed the enemy as if automatic, punching Bullet clean in the face. "Hey! Hey!" I remember Uncle saying as he and others rushed to intervene, but not before Bullet smacked me back, spliff flying out my mouth, with both of us falling to the ground fighting.

When we were separated Uncle decided he would raise his voice as if to restore order, whilst 'Bullet' was trying to

**109**

articulate self-defence. Me; I felt like a king, I was happy, everything seemed to make sense, my actions made me feel no longer a puppet, as I picked up my spliff, dusted myself off with a puffed out chest still relatively silent. I was no longer in awe of Uncle but of my team and the job we did; that's what was important, the job we did in the midst of such a tough time.

"Him a bloodclaart traitor, wha u bring him back over yah fa. You disrespect the whole team man, fuckery you deal wid".

With Dad now looking over to us from the Landrover smiling through his dark shades, Uncle still ranting and everybody else shook not knowing what to do, I simply turned my back, nodded at Jaden to come and we marched off with the crew, back to the yard to go roll another giant spliff of Columbian; nobody daren't follow us.

# OUT FOR JUSTICE

It turned out that mum was leaving dad and had never actually intended to return to Antigua. She sent a letter to Dad saying she was divorcing him, that's my memory of mum's confirmation of her departure. I commend dad for telling us as it must have been a difficult thing for him to deal with emotionally and as a teenager sometimes you don't take these things on board; I know I didn't.

At this point in my life I was too smoked out, angry and too busy hustling ganja. I felt sorry for my sister really as her being a young lady was practically left to be raised by dad and that was difficult. I never blamed mum in fact I backed her decision. As much as I love my pops I never could understand why he would hit my mother the way he did at times as she was such a lovely person. I remember the last time he did; I must have been 15 and a half. I remember the commotion, mum screaming and me plucking up the courage to go to her aid.

I remember seeing mum on the floor, a thick wooden stick snapped besides her and her looking up at me crying, tears streaming down her face. I remember what she said to me. I remember what I said to Dad at the time too, that if he ever put his hands on her again I would kill him and I really meant it so I was happy she decided to bounce, because he didn't deserve her in my opinion.

Me, Jaden and Hawa never did ever talk collectively about mum leaving, we kind of just got on with things. Now as I said I was in a very dark place during this period of time but at the same time this is my most reflective. A famous poet once said 'Inside you there's an artist you don't know about'. I was about to discover the artist I was.

After the fight between me and Bullet a mutual respect was gained; though he ultimately did get back his roll. I was now deputy and Jaden retained his roll meaning Bullet literally had to look over his shoulder. In fact it was still as if we ran things, as anything we wanted to do we did and in the end, Bullet really only dealt with Star of David, Empress Africa and Black Silk.

We dealt with all the other horses and I still coordinated the training programmes for those horses I was in control of. It was at this time that Uncle decided to buy a wild young chestnut horse which came from a strong bloodline of successful racers. Apparently Uncle paid good money for the pony which he brought from a guy called Shadow. The thing was this pony really was wild! You remember how I told you how Brian Lara dispatched of the English? Well, this pony was dispatching anybody that went near it!! Breaking a young horse was something I wasn't familiar with.

"Wha dem a do to the horse Chineman" I remember asking on one occasion.

**113**

"Dem a break it, the horse young it never have a saddle, nobody ever ride it but it ready fi ride so it need breaking" Chineman would say.

"Oh right".

I would be getting on with the more advanced stable duties I was now familiar with. I remember seeing sometimes 3, 4, 5 men around this young horse which was tied to a rope, trying all kinds of crazy manuvours to get the horse to obey them, but then time and time again getting defeated by the horse. He was a feisty creature, pretty ugly too, but he had balls!

I remember seeing one of our jockeys managing to get on its back bareback but then getting flung off high into the sky and landing plump on his back, I remember the little young ugly horse railing up and kicking guys in their heads for fun. I remember the guys with planks of wood beating the horse still to no avail and thinking 'what the fuck are these evil guys doing to the poor thing'.

I remember that this would go on for days with the guys always losing the battle. What use to amaze me most was that these guys were mostly professional guys; you're talking Bullet, Jockeys, and Horsemen with even Uncle chipping in at times. As the days went by I was more and more agitated to intervene.

Eventually after a week or so of provocation, beatings and taunting; cruelty manifested with the horse being tied to a tree in isolation on the courtyard; he must have been left for around another week without any water, food and had eaten all the grass within its vicinity leaving the area nothing but a barren patch. He was literally left to starve but I was not about to let this happen.

I remember approaching Uncle and asking him what he was doing with the horse. His response, "me a left it fi dead man, the horse too wild, it fucking crazy man, we cyan do nuttin wid dat dey".

My response was simple…………………..

"Give me the horse".

Uncle looked at me quite perplexed, then let off a nervous chuckle, "hehe, you want the horse" pausing for a couple seconds before asking "wha u go do wid the horse?".

My response "Mek it a winner"

Uncle looked at me with a more serious look on his face before turning his back and swaggering off to his jeep saying "Hear dis, mind the horse don't kill you, you can't keep it here".

Deep in my mind I knew he wouldn't say no, "Dat cool man, respect yeah" I said.

Finally before driving off Uncle leaned out the window and shouted "You have a name fe it?"

Indeed I did, his name was "Out for Justice".

# BEAUTY AND THE BEAST

You see horses are just like people; emotional with their own characteristics. Every animal has its own personality and once you figure out his her personality you can form a mutual respect, build a working relationship.

My Aunt Cassie's husband Steady had a horse stable close to theirs and this is where I ended up taking 'Justice'. He had been through so much in a short space of time he was emaciated, shot for confidence and easily spooked. I remember when I untied him from the tree he was chained too and the looks and laughter I got off of everybody I passed whilst taking him across the village.

"Where u a tek dat deh freedom, wha it be a horse, bwoy dat look dead no fuck".

This was the general consensus from most people I encountered when I first got 'Justice'. The thing was, here was just another animal for me to rescue, like back in the day before moving to Antigua, Jungle Masters; where my friends would bring any injured, abandoned animals to my house for me to look after due to my connect with the RSPCA; it was just that we didn't have the RSPCA over here!!

For the first few days looking after 'Justice' I didn't even try to touch him in anyway, getting him into the single isolated stable which was going to be his new home was a case of tricking him into the stable and then quickly jumping over the stable door, shit scared this horse would lash out at me. I made sure he had all the basic amenities needed for his keep, fresh water, fresh grass

**117**

which I would cut myself and I would take hard food from the Race Yard knowing Uncle wouldn't couldnt really say anything about it.

There was a pile of sand which me and my friends had visited earlier with a wheel barrow and had used for the bedding of the stable in case 'Justice' wanted to lie down, the horse was real comfortable.

I would give him more food than he needed, more grass than he needed and fresh water. We would have to get him out the stable initially to do this due to his erratic nature and fear of people, tugging on his lead early days he never attempted to bolt off or anything he would lazily walk out his stable, he was happy being lead.

So the routine was set; tending to my horse I was now spending more time away from the race yard only turning up to groom the horses I was responsible for with me and Jaden rotating duties to cater for our new asset, it wasn't difficult at all.

After finishing at the race yard we would loiter around 'Justice' stable puffing ganja, hustling and talking loud same way until late night sometimes. As people got to know it was my horse, I would eventually be able to leave duties in the hands of trusted friends who would turn 'Justice' out when needed or move him to a fresh spot of grass.

Lunch times I would go visit my horse or just observe him as he was simply across the football pitch. As the weeks went by of doing the same thing, I wasn't so nervous around Justice, he wasn't so nervous around me, he was also looking a lot better physically. The first time I actually stroked him was a good feeling, I remember it clearly.

Leaning over the stable door, he was taking it easy having being turned out all day. Munching on grass he looked up at me, "Justice wha agwan big man? Come?" I called out to him gently; direct. He had this thing about him where he would play Oh I'm not listening but I really am', on that occasion he didn't flinch at all; though I knew he was now aware of my voice and listening as it was only us two and his left ear rotated in my direction. "Justice? Come?" I said again;  this time he looked over at me, but held firm.

I decided to get some hard food from the feeding area in a tin and enter his stable, locking the door behind me. "Justice you want some more food, come?", shaking the tin lightly; he understood what this meant. On this occasion 'Justice' stopped munching the grass he was eating and looked up at me directly 'eye to eye', here I was thinking 'ok so what you going to do?', either this horse was going to kill me or realise that I was different from everybody else he had come into contact with and respect what I'd done for him.

I wasn't nervous at all, I trusted my own judgement; slowly whilst I had his attention, I calmly took some food out of the tin pan in my hand. "Justice, if you want this you going to have to come for it", I said gently all the whilst remaining resilient but friendly in body posture; I respected this was his environment, where he had come to feel safe, it was up to him to decide in his time what was in his best interests.

After an intense stare off, semi – heavy panting 'Justice' ignored me, turned around and picked up another bunch of grass. I put the hard food back in the tin; still didn't give up and simply decided to wait for him. Again he watched me, I shook the tin pan again, "Come on justice, look at this lovely hard food you don't want that grass you want this"; friendly posture, big smiles, again he twisted his neck to look at me, swaying his head as if not sure whether to trust me.

A few seconds later he turned back to face me and without any indication walked over to me put his muzzle in the tin and accepted the treat on offer. The sense of achievement was overwhelming and though I had to withhold that feeling giving the position I was in, I will never forget it. I'd managed to do what nobody else had; got to within stroking distance of this horse without getting damaged.

**LETS GO SHOP**

People where either puzzled or amazed thinking how on earth did I achieve what all others couldn't? Me and my horse became such good buddies in the end I could go to the shop with him following me loose!! Yeah I mean, no head collar, no rope, nothing. 'Justice' was more like 'Scooby Doo'!! If I went into the shop he would simply stare at the entrance, let off a few neighs until I came out; it was amazing. It got so crazy that if I was walking down the road with 'Justice', if I started to skip he would trot and if I ran he would keep up with me never opting to run past me just stay with me. We had a unique relationship and people were starting to recognise.

The horse was now a well-known celebrity of the village. One incident which did not go down well though but will be forever remembered by me was when I took him to my Aunts house for a drink. Justice was drinking from a bucket which was placed under an outdoor tap connected to my Aunts house; whilst drinking he got spooked by something and bolted at such speed he ripped the head of the tap clean off the pipe, water was spraying everywhere, grandma was going hysterical and I can admit that was the last time the horse was allowed there that's for sure!!

Once I'd made that breakthrough, 'Justice' was so easy to manage; he loved young people; loved being groomed; loved the attention and put quite simply, behaved more like a dog than a horse. After a period of good care, everybody could see that 'Justice' was looking better and better. Most people whom hadn't seen him for a while would comment "A de same horse dat deh?", stunned with the progress 'Justice' had made under my provision and care. Word even got to Uncle and upon visualising the progress himself he soon invited me to house 'Justice' back at Cedar View Race Yard, an invitation I accepted without hesitation.

You see my aspirations as explained from when I got the horse was to turn 'Justice' into a winner and I knew that in order for even more progress to be made he would have to learn new traits.

I was impressed with how comfortable 'Justice' was embracing his new environment; I situated him next to 'Distant Relative' in 'Black Silks' stable. Due to the injury 'Black Silk' had recovered from it was deemed better for him to move to the racetrack where there were also stables; being closer to the racetrack meant he could train more consistently on the track better preparing him for race day conditions which was what he needed right about now.

Justice' new environment seemed to give him fantastic confidence; in no time at all he seemed to turn from straggly colt into strapping young stallion; everybody was telling me his confirmation and bloodline meant I should definitely consider him for racing. 'Distant Relative' was a great mentor and in no time at all with my assistance 'Justice' was broken, being ridden in saddle and in light training with 'Distant Relative' and how majestic he moved.

**123**

Now besides working on the race yard, having studied Jah Bless, myself and Jaden were hustling relentlessly; 17 and 16 years old growing up in Antigua this and horses was all we knew; this was life. With 'Justice' settled and more secure, it was time to step up the grind and as such over the next few months; me and bro were now more or less controlling the flow of marijuana in 7 villages, 5 within our immediate vicinity with clients ranging from other dope dealers, the average joe bloggs, rasta's, to corrupt police.

# CARNIVAL TIME

Now this would not be a true Caribbean story without a touch of Carnival. Despite our gangster lifestyle we had many fantastic times in Wadadli and one of the most wonderful moments everybody looked forward to would be the islands Carnival. In fact it makes me laugh when people outside of the West Indies say they have been or are going to the carnival. In my opinion, you have not experienced a Caribbean Carnival if you haven't lived in the Caribbean or been on holiday to the West Indies and witnessed it first-hand. I say this for a number of reasons which I will explain.

First of all, in my village all the manz dem would start practicing dance routines at least a month before carnival late at night. Every year we had different themes and songs; Soca music battles would commence well before carnival and the tunes that were deemed hot would spark off mass crazy dance moves that would be copied throughout the Soca infested islands every year. Drinks flowing, new tunes, new moves, you had the man dem who would be the dancing type and you had the laid back guys who would be the Shanti town type. However during the practice nights drink guzzlers and weed smokers would come together in celebration.

The Wadadli Carnival is approximately 9 days long, 9 days long!! It would work like this………. Young men in particular would leave their village on Day One of the Carnival and would not be seen again unless it was to return home to have a wash, change clothes and then you would be gone again. We would dance for days on end and because Uncle had a yard close to the city centre we would often go to his for a wash and then bounce off. For the last 2 carnivals I attended in Antigua I remember coming home on the last day looking like zombies, smoked out, skin white, stale sweat and stinking!; the only time you could get away looking and smelling like that!

Shanti Town; this is where the gangsters would meet. Shanti town ran all night for the duration of the Carnival; Carnival was a very productive time and we would max out on weed sales during this time. If you knew how to move it was a great place to chill, here is where you would find all the sound systems, and experience your sound clashes. Crucifix against Stonewall, Stone Love against Kilimanjaro, Tony Matterhorn, Poison Dart, yeah the coolest of the coolest met here and this was the place you would go to bump and grind your girl, to look for a grind or to buy a draw.

Lions Den was the opposite of Shanti Town in that it was a Soca pepperpot for those who were not into the dark, moody, smokey atmosphere, though equally as intense but for different reasons. A sexually charged sweat fest full of testosterone and oestrogen, pretty young ladies in the shortest of shorts, bright colours and guys like peacocks puffing out their chests dancing trying to attract these young ladies with their boisterous displays.

Everybody would have a handkerchief or rag to help repel the sweat which would drip as a result of endless dancing to the sounds of local band Burning Flames, and local artists like Claudette Peters and Mighty Sparrow. "SWINGING ENGINE, SWINGING ENGINE ALL NIGHT, IN SHE GEARBOX IN SHE GEARBOX ALL NIGHT!" the sounds would ring out from the speakers!!. Lions was a real Soca Frenzy for young people to party throughout the night.

The famous Iron band; if we ever needed to find Dad he would be here. In these days you didn't have a mobile phone so trying to find a person amongst hundreds of thousands of carnival attendees would be difficult; however looking for Dad he would always be here!! Without failure, he would be found banging his piece of metal with his crew, a whole parade of them marching around the city centre to a joyous sound. It was quite incredible the tunes which could be generated from the scrap metal the troopers would bang together.

The most dramatic part of the Carnival, 'J'ouvert Morning' which began at 7am, people from all villages jamming their way to town, both young and old, people jamming jamming jamming unlike anything you would have experienced, totally uninhibited, intoxicated with something, hypnotized too this wild music, gyal whining up on man, man whining up on gyal, trains of people just all whining up, at times it got very sexual but then all fun and within Caribbean reason!!

**128**

In scenery of splattered colour, during this morning of utter madness in certain parade troops many people would get injured, people would climb buildings and dive off into the crowds, if you were luck you would escape without getting smashed in the face with a bucket of paint or water thrown over you!!

I remember one of the most unreal things I'd ever seen in my life happened one of these mornings; a man dancing through the crowd as if possessed in a particular troop with a 'Pigs Head' on a pole!!! The song went something like this ……………………………..

"PIG FOOT AND PIG MOUT, EVERYBODY SHOUT OUT!!!"

"PIG FOOT AND PIG MOUT, EVERYBODY SHOUT OUT!!!"

Now I know you are thinking 'What the' and yes experiencing a real Caribbean Carnival will give you many 'What the' moments; certain elements; days are not for the faint hearted, but the 'Caribbean Carnival that I know; there is simply one word to describe it;

"Immense".

**GUNPLAY**

Back end of 1996 life was moving too fast; for young people we knew way too much and were moving way to dangerous. Despite this I would say I still was a very focused young man and as such school was not a problem for me personally. I understood the importance education would play in my future and so apart from maths I loved all subjects and in the end came out of school with exceptionally good grades; 7 O levels all A - C.

Around this time, government was getting more radical on the 'war on drugs', Uncle's empire was coming under increased pressure from the police and within a short space of time we had been raided twice within a couple of weeks. On each occasion packages were found and as such Uncle had to post up fines to the tune of 450,000 dollars and 250,000 dollars equivalent to £450k and £250k respectively.

Jah Bless had returned from the states after a few months. He returned to find out that his secret 'Herb Plantation' had been raided by the army! I remember them driving past our yard in huge lorry's full of the giant marijuana plants we had helped grow and harvest. Shaking my head in disappointment I just thought about the money we would lose because of this.

Border control was getting tighter and tighter and as such it was becoming more and more difficult to get marijuana to the island. Payment from Uncle for looking after the

**131**

horses was getting more and more inconsistent and even though we was hustling for him that money was usually reinvested in more herb with a portion of it having to be paid back to him. Furthermore, the fact we were not doing as well as we previously were on the racetrack meant that Uncles outgoings were higher than usual and it was affecting him, us, everybody; people were suffering.

Sensing difficulties ahead, me and jaden at one point decided to take matters into our own hands. We decided that if Uncle wasn't going to pay us our worth then we would take our worth in herb from his secret spot on the yard. Late at night we orchestrated a move which seen us smuggle a 20kg key of Columbian weed from his stash.

We had a good link, a local rastaman who would move the weed for us and then pay us at the end of the week. The plan was to remain low-key and that I did; for Jaden however you could say it was harder to resist temptation, he decided with his first return on that key that a Super Nintendo and the hottest Nike Air Raid trainers were small luxury's needed, who could blame him I mean he was still only 16!

It was a good idea to take that key because since I had turned 16 Dad slowly weaned himself off of looking after me and I more or less had to fend for myself. His philosophy was that from 16 we were men who kinda had to look after ourselves and the key of weed helped us do this during difficult times.

Talking of difficult times; with still quite a lot of the key to be shifted a 'drought' hit us again. When a drought hits things get hectic. Dad wasn't too happy that we were doing better than him hustling weed; hustlers were getting robbed at gunpoint left, right and centre by other hustlers; the price of weed was going up, these were dangerous times; however as drastic as things got me and Jaden never felt threatened at all.

We had come to hear that the hustlers out robbing other hustlers were our good friends 'twin Rasta Brothers', Rasai and Manyah, we thought they were cool guys and why they decided to switch on everybody we would never know. However just for added protection both me and Jaden by now had pistols, two huge aggressive pitbull terriers, Blood and Cally Bud.

Jaden during our time here had mastered the art of pitbull training and so both dogs were trained to attack anybody with a simple command. On occasions we would go practice shooting in the fields behind the stables, with a particular tree bearing the brunt of our excitement and train our pitbulls using cattle chains, car tyres and other accessories that Jaden deemed necessary for 'Pitbull Personal Development'!.

By the grace of God, it never got to the point where we would have to buss our guns or stick up anybody because we already had a reputation and the family was already notoriously known; however there were occasions when a man would have to get pistol whipped for being late with money or put simply 'taking the piss'.

I remember an occasion when we traded a brand new encased pistol with silencer for 'a key' of Columbian. Brand new, it was beautifully laid out in a black wooden box, with purple, red and black velvet interior. The most successful hustlers avoid drawing attention and so though we done the deal, we never actually used the gun and simply traded it to another hustler for some 2200ec dollars which we used to get more herb.

We were going on real bad, thinking like bosses, hurricane season was just coming to a conclusion and though we had survived quite a mean tropical storm named 'Iris', my biggest memory during these times was the announcement of the death of one of our biggest Hip Hop musical influences 'Tupac 'Amaru' Shakur'.

# BUJU, BERES AND VIVIAN RICHARDS

Wadadli culture had a huge influence on us three personally. Up to now my accent is still very different from other members of my family who live in the UK due to my experiences. Embracing reggae but still down with hip hop, I'd met quite a few well - known artists from Jamaica visiting Wadadli being connected to Uncle.

It wasn't uncommon popping down to 'The Don's' other yard near the beach and bumping into Buju Banton, Beres Hammond, Freddie Mcgregor and the likes. Uncle had connections; if I told you what some of these artists got up to at the yard you'd be surprised! Though it was another surprise during 1996 that made me think about whom I was, what I was becoming, and where my life was heading.

It must have been like 3pm in the afternoon, we was chilling in the yard making sales as we did in between popping over to the stables to tend to duties. Anyhow we was all chilling smoking the highest grade. We had Blood and Cally Bud; patrolling the yard in case of police; pit bulls in the Caribbean like in England were illegal and as such the police were entitled to shoot them on sight if they were seen loitering on streets or were not chained to their kennels in yards. However I'd never known an occasion where this may have happened and our dogs ran free all the time.

We always hustled from the back of the yard; we'd heard a car pull up and instinctively our dogs rushed off barking wildly to find out who was looking to possibly enter or intrude. They were trained this way, this was normal practice as if it was police this stalling tactic would give us enough time to breeze out.

Who could it be? If our dogs were familiar with you they wouldn't bat an eyelid, they'd been trained to attack police or intruders, dogs have a good sense of smell, so obviously whoever they were, were either unfamiliar, intruders or police. I went to find out whilst the manz dem got ready to breeze.

I didn't recognise them at first, 3 guys in a jeep, looked like a rental. One of them had got out to enter the yard but daren't having met the guards. "Assalaamu Alaikum who's that, is that you LT?" said the unfamiliar. I'd now recognised the voice and face and the others; it was; it was our cousins Abdul, Hamza and Nicky from Leicester, England.

"What you saying cuzzy? Yo call dem dogs back man how you got dem big ugly dogs running around the garden like that man. Suppose I entered the garden I'd be dead, bloody heck man" said Abdul.

He was right, it was that serious had he entered the yard he would have been dog food literally!

It was an amazing feeling seeing these guys; they were over here on holiday and had come to look for us. Over the next few days we spent a lot of time together. We

**137**

took them horse riding, we went for drives, Abdul was a smoker so joined us smoking the highest grade; we generally had a major catch-up.

Abdul and Hamza were brothers whilst Nicky was their cousin but not ours though his family was considered family anyway. His mother lived over here too. I remember rolling with Abdul and Nicky the following day after they came to check us and how we ended up at Vivian 'Viv' Richards house. Nicky's mother was good friends with the former Cricket Legends wife and was at the house. Nicky needed to see her about suttin and as such we ended up at his house.

I remember being in awe of his yard and in his presence. I remember on one occasion how a spontaneous conversation developed about how me and Abdul and a lot of our family were Muslims. For some reason Nicky's mother and Viv's wife found it hilarious, but out of nowhere Viv backed them up by explaining how Muslims were some of the most pious people he had ever met, particularly in the countries he had visited and worked in; it was a good feeling having his support on an island where this was virtually non – existent.

**HOME**

Wadadli life made us resilient, tough, streetwise, but ultimately the teachings of our parents still kept us grounded. I say that in that, for my 16th birthday, my birthday present was an ounce of Jamaican weed from my Dad. This was his mentality and this was how we was living. Dad always said to me that if I was to do any drugs to 'smoke ganja' and nothing else.

He taught us to shun cigarettes, crack, heroine and any other drugs and I'm proud to say that, that upbringing today, means that though I have experimented with marijuana for a long time on major levels; I no longer smoke at all and have never to this day experimented with any other drugs except cigarettes and very late alcohol.

With regards to the debate on the legalisation of Cannabis I would argue in favour of it being decriminalised; regards other drugs particularly 'Class A' my views are very different. I'll explain why………

I always believed that Uncle was just a 'Weed man' with regards to him being called 'Don'; over time I'd come to realise this was not the case at all. Uncle was in fact a skilled drug dealer, a much darker person than we realised who was capable of adapting to suit his circumstances. Rumour has it that he was in fact a hard drug user in his early days before becoming a so called 'Don'.

Being familiar and wiser I'd come to realise that those flashbacks of 'Uncle' cooking up crack in our kitchen were actually real. I'd come to realise that apart from 'Me, Jaden, Hawa, Dad and the rest of our immediate family' more or less everybody else was in fact on crack cocaine and this was why Uncle had so much power over them. The thing with 'Crack' in the Caribbean is that it is what you could say very clean and as such it can be very hard to even detect if somebody was on it, though they would be equally as dependent as anybody else on it.

His henchmen were literally paid in crack that was the realisation. Dad had always been totally against crack and over time himself began to overstand even more how this drug fucked up people's lives, with him coming to realise many of his friends were actually dying off of this shit. It affected him deeply and his relationship with his brother was becoming strained, even though he tried to maintain.

You see those 'big tings' Uncle had promised never really materialised. Uncle was apparently supposed to let my Dad control a 'Lumber Yard' he planned to set up distributing lumber from Guyana, green heart and purple heart timber, but this only happened when it was too late.

Rina must have seen something before we did because from the beginning of 1996 she and the kids had scarped to Atlanta, Georgia in the knowledge that Uncle was banned from entering the United States. Myself and her kind of didn't get along once we'd settled in, we found her really stuck up her own ass,  but the kids, man when they left it was heart-breaking.

I also remember how a family in our village barred a pretty young lady from seeing me simply because I was the 'Don's nephew. She had come to visit family from the U.K, London, England and so of course we struck up a friendship instantly. She wasn't the prettiest thing but her accent, the way she was, reminded me of so much I was familiar with. It was heart wrenching when she was barred from associating with me as she loved our movements and when I used to take her back to my place. Charmaine I think her name was.

'Justice' my horse eventually did have a race just the one, and though he didn't win he came second from 3 racers; the fact he raced under my name through me being granted officially my licence to train made me very proud. Historically at the time I was the youngest professional 'Horse Trainer' on the island at 17, I still have the licence to this day issued by the Antiguan Turf Club. 'Justice's' career was short lived however, I made the mistake of getting caught up in the hype of his explosive start and allowed 'Bullet' through Uncle and some twits he knew down at the race track over work him.

Being a young horse he suffered a career ending injury and so I eventually sold him to a new riding school on the other side of the island. I would say this heart wrenching incident, the lifestyle we were living at the time and the fact Uncle was now taking more risks with pushing 'Crack Cocaine' made me realise something.

It was time to go home.

**142**

# LOVE ETERNAL

Thoughts of returning to the UK were more intense after finishing school summer 1996. I guess it was that feeling of asking yourself 'What are you going to do with your life now?' School seemed to give an unbalanced life balance and as such not having it seemed to destabilise me even further for a while.

What could I do? All I cared about was 'making money from ganja and horses'. For 6 months I simply looked after my horses, me and Uncle had brought a new racer from Miami called 'Positive'; money I received from 'Justice' I basically reinvested in this animal; she did well at first but also suffered an injury later on which reduced her appearances and performance. In the end we put her out to stud so as to make some local ponies for the future.

About March 1997 by chance I'd managed to find an Agricultural College Course close to my village that specialised in Agricultural business. It was ran by a Canadian Christian Ministry but thoughts of its background didn't actually come to mind.

The main tutor was a white Canadian dude called Dennis Axelquist we became very good friends, he was a much focused calm individual and easy to relate to. Being around him seemed to remind me of England, of everybody who attended the college he was most intrigued by my business idea which was to upgrade my Cedar View Race Yard as a major commercial brand in the Equestrian World and expand it to have my own equestrian businesses.

I took him to visit my Cedar View Race Yard and he was blown away by my equestrian intellect, the amount of responsibility I had at such a young age and the life he had come to know I was living at the time. Dennis believed in order for me to realise my dream of becoming a major influence in the equestrian world, I had no option but to leave Antigua; he said in no uncertain terms that either I leave the island to further my ambition, end up in jail or end up dead; by this time I was however of the same opinion.

Dennis advised either I return to England to undertake Equine Studies or move to another country where there was a big equestrian industry such as Canada, America, the Middle East and so on where I could further my equestrian education. After the course had finished Dennis asked me to stay on voluntarily for a few hours a week and assist him delivering seminars to schools and Business Conferences promoting Agricultural business; it was a brilliant experience.

After a few months Dennis decided to return to Canada, I would never hear from him or see him again. Anyhow, the foundations had been laid; I needed to make a decision! For a while I toyed with the idea of America, or maybe Canada before realising the only place 'worthy of consideration' was England.

**145**

Family, friends, Leicester, the U.K's equine industry, me; there were so many reasons why I needed to return to the UK. These times I was very much thinking for myself, escaping Wadadli, in my opinion Uncle owed me money due to the fact he fucked up my horse 'Justice', brought another horse which was virtually a crock, and even though she was to be bred, though and I would benefit indirectly, I needed money now.

"Uncle me a look fi go back England you know, u owe me some money" I would say.

"Me owe you money wha mek u feel me owe u money?" he would respond.

"Because unuh people dem fuck up my horse and den you gone go buy a fuck up horse waste off my money; I want to go back to learn about horses on the highest level so can come back, set up Cedar View and clean up; I want to dominate England too"

We could talk on this level now after all we had been through and as he knew I was never one to kiss ass.

"Freedom if you want to go back to England that is not a problem, me will handle that for you" he chuckled lightly.

"No sah this is what we go do. Me go tek off, I will pay for me and I will tek off in say the next month or so. You can pay for Hawa and we will split the cost of Jaden I don't want him using his own money; tru dem still in a school just for the summer still".

Jaden and Hawa were still in school and so if they were to return they could only come for holiday during the summer break, I however wanted to leave as soon as possible as my intentions were to look into attending an Equine College somewhere in the UK.

Breaking the news to Jaden and Hawa was more difficult than breaking the news to my Dad. By the time I was due to leave me and Dad had a very complex, strained relationship. We were growing up, he still tried to rule with an iron fist; after an argument where I walked out of a family meeting he organised for dubious reasons, I had to 'fold him up' in self-defence after he lashed out at me; we've never been quite the same.

I remember on the occasion how he ran for his gun threatening to shoot me because I embarrassed him so bad! You should have seen how I scattered!! Anyhow, we are great now, love him eternal and he's actually in his old age mellowed beyond belief, a very caring man with an envious relationship with his now grandchildren; how ironic.

Jaden and Hawa accepted the fact that I needed to return home. I always had at the back of my mind that they would follow suit but as stated needed to finish school first. With how we were raised I didn't leave my bro with any advice, just to look after himself, stay focused and look out for the horses and that if he ever wanted to return to the UK for good to let me know; let Jah guide as Jah Bless would say; for Hawa, very much the same.

**147**

**ONE LOVE WADADLI**

It's funny how when you reflect back on life and read certain signs, depending on how life is treating you, determines how you interpret those signs! Well the day before I left 'Rainbow Melody' had her first foal, I viewed this as a sign of prosperity, great things ahead.

The time had come for me to leave; like the day I left England I can't remember too much about the day I left Wadadli except the above and a few other things. The things that really do stick are feelings; I had a feeling of relief; relief in that I knew the life I'd been living was no life a normal teenager should have experienced. However I was 19 now and despite many hard ships I'd grown to except and embrace who I was, who we were and the life we had come to live; I mean what else could I have done?

I felt I'd made this decision at the right time and looked forward to another chapter of my life and returning back to the UK. Many things were running through my head the last few weeks in Dadli such as 'What would I return too?', 'How would I fit back in?', 'Would I remember everyone? 'Who would remember me?', 'What things may have changed?'.

I was thinking about the weather and how I was looking forward to the 4 seasons; the wind, rain, even the snow in those winters. Being in a multicultural society, I remember wanting to see 'Asian ,White, Chinese people; all the gyal I would link, mixed race 'tings' who we called over here in

Dadli, butterskin gyal', would pop into my head expressed through a radiant smile across my face.

The English accent; I would laugh at how I would be back amongst my English speaking peeps and used to mimic speaking like them again. The busy roads, buses and top cars; Heathrow airport, I thought about it all.

I do remember going to my cousin 'Cashew Nut's' girlfriends house to get my afro cane-rowed and how neat and handsome I looked. Though excited I knew that deep down it was also a very sad time; working at the stables for the last time was difficult and saying goodbye to the horses was real tough. I loved these animals. I went to visit 'Justice' at his new home and seeing him doing so well made me feel good in that if he could embrace a new environment in such confidence so could I.

Even in this time I remained focused; speaking again on the last day to my blood kin Jaden regards doing well at school, exams and 'running tings' with the crew; emotional times but it wasn't within us to show it. Uncle gave me a lift to catch the plane, I wore my baggy jeans, Basketball top Jah Bless gave me and Nike Air Barrage Trainers, whilst smoking that last spliff of Jamaican, I was ready.

And you know as dramatic, abusive and challenging as my life was between the ages of 14 and 19, there isn't one thing I regret. I loved the fact my Uncle was the 'Don'; if it wasn't for him I would have never had the opportunity to work with racehorses and become a trainer; I loved the fact nothing was easy because if you can go through what we did and still come out with positive experiences and a head held high, then anything is possible.

So what lies ahead? Jah knows, but what I do know is that horses saved my life and for that I'm forever grateful to these majestic creatures, in my opinion 'man's best friend'.

So back to LE2, Leicester.

One Love Wadadli, 'Ras-Mus' wheel out; Salaams.

In loving memory of Urcin (Iron Sheikh) Martin
(R)ise (I)n (P)ower
21st March 1968 - 4th May 2015.

Special thanks has to go out to my brother Irfan Chhatbar whom without his artistry much of my magic would not be possible.

'Coming Soon 'From The Hood 2 Horses LE2'

28316069R00085

Printed in Great Britain
by Amazon